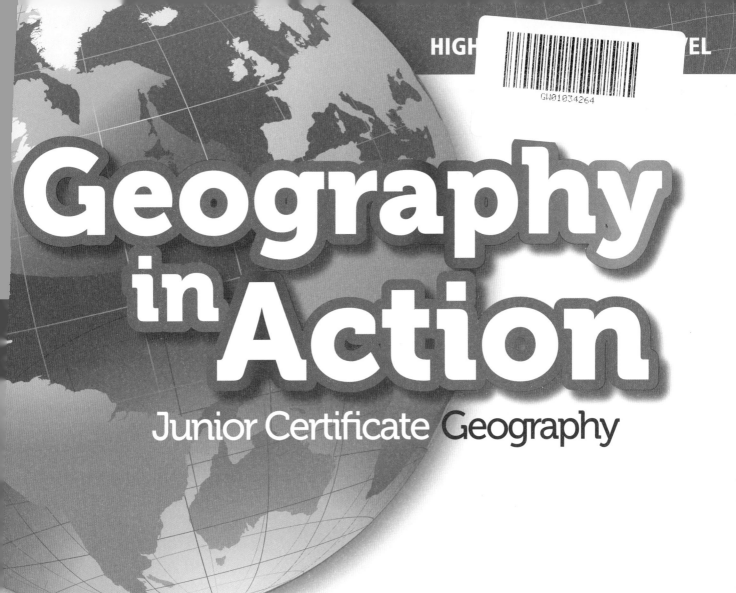

Geography in Action

Junior Certificate Geography

Activity Book

Norma Lenihan
Jason O'Brien

educate.ie

Published by:

Educate.ie

Walsh Educational Books Ltd
Castleisland, Co. Kerry, Ireland

www.educate.ie

Printed and bound by:

Walsh Colour Print, Castleisland

ISBN: 978-1-910468-47-0

The authors and publisher would like to thank Ordnance Survey Ireland and Peter Barrow for permission to reproduce maps and photographs.

Ordnance Survey Ireland Permit No. 9006

© Ordnance Survey Ireland/Government of Ireland

National Mapping Agency - www.osi.ie

Contents

When you have completed a topic, it is important to check what you have learned and how well you have understood it. It is also important to plan when you will review each topic in future.

The traffic light system

Use the traffic light system to help you check your learning and understanding of each topic. Each time you review a topic, choose the colour that most closely matches how you feel about what you have learned. Review each topic and tick your level until you get to green, and record the date of the review.

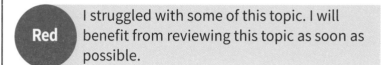

Red — I struggled with some of this topic. I will benefit from reviewing this topic as soon as possible.

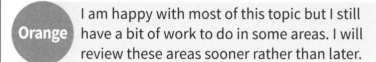

Orange — I am happy with most of this topic but I still have a bit of work to do in some areas. I will review these areas sooner rather than later.

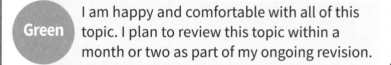

Green — I am happy and comfortable with all of this topic. I plan to review this topic within a month or two as part of my ongoing revision.

Economic Activities: 1
Focus on the primary sector

- I can list the three types of economic activity.

  Review ●●● (/ /); Review ●●● (/ /); Review ●●● (/ /)

- I can explain the difference between renewable and non-renewable resources and give examples of each.

  Review ●●● (/ /); Review ●●● (/ /); Review ●●● (/ /)

- I can explain how a local water supply works.

  Review ●●● (/ /); Review ●●● (/ /); Review ●●● (/ /)

- I can explain what an irrigation scheme is.

  Review ●●● (/ /); Review ●●● (/ /); Review ●●● (/ /)

- I can name and locate an oil-producing country.

  Review ●●● (/ /); Review ●●● (/ /); Review ●●● (/ /)

- I can describe the different stages of peat exploitation.

  Review ●●● (/ /); Review ●●● (/ /); Review ●●● (/ /)

- I can explain why overfishing occurs.

  Review ●●● (/ /); Review ●●● (/ /); Review ●●● (/ /)

- I can describe three measures to stop overfishing.

  Review ●●● (/ /); Review ●●● (/ /); Review ●●● (/ /)

- I can describe how farming is a system of inputs, processes and outputs.

  Review ●●● (/ /); Review ●●● (/ /); Review ●●● (/ /)

1. Define the following terms:

(a) Economic activities

_____

_____

(b) Primary economic activities

_____

_____

(c) Secondary economic activities

_____

_____

(d) Tertiary economic activities

_____

_____

(e) Natural resources

_____

_____

(f) Renewable resources

_____

_____

(g) Non-renewable resources

_____

_____

2. Local water supply

Name a local water supply you have studied.	
What river does the water come from?	
How much water is produced each day?	
Why is filtering used?	
Explain why chemicals are added to the water. Name two of these chemicals.	
Where is the water then stored?	
How does the water get to our taps?	

3. What is irrigation?

_____

_____

4. Irrigation schemes

Name an irrigation scheme you have studied.	
Why was an irrigation scheme needed in this area?	
Describe the stages of building this irrigation scheme.	
Explain two advantages of this scheme.	
Explain two disadvantages of this scheme.	

5. Why should we conserve oil?

_____

_____

_____

6. Can you list four ways oil may be used by you and your family?

(a) _____

(b) _____

(c) _____

(d) _____

7. Explain two advantages of using oil as an energy source.

(a) _____

(b) _____

8. Explain two disadvantages of using oil as an energy source.

(a) _____

(b) _____

9. Oil-producing countries

Name an oil-producing country.	
Describe two ways this country has benefitted from producing oil.	
Name two locations of oil and gas deposits in Ireland.	

10. Bogs

(a) Name the instrument that was used in the past for cutting turf.

_____

(b) Explain three differences between raised and blanket bogs.

_____

_____

_____

(c) Name the government-established body responsible for Ireland's peat bogs.

_____

(d) Match the correct machine with its function.

Machine		Function
Harrow		Used to dry out the loose peat on the surface
Grader		Gathers the loose dried peat into ridges
Ridger		Used to dig drains and dry out the bog
Miller		Levels the bog
Ditcher		Scrapes loose a thin layer on top of the bog

11. Cut-away bogs

(a) What are cut-away bogs?

_____

_____

(b) Describe three reasons why cut-away bogs are ideal locations for wind farms.

_____

_____

_____

(c) List three other possible uses for cut-away bogs.

_____

_____

_____

12. List five types of renewable energy.

(a) _____

(b) _____

(c) _____

(d) _____

(e) _____

13. Describe and explain three reasons for overfishing.

(a) _____

_____

(b) _____

_____

(c) _____

_____

14. Describe and explain three measures taken to limit the amount of fish being caught.

(a) _____

_____

(b) _____

_____

(c) _____

_____

15. Farming

Inputs	Processes	Outputs

16. Crossword

ACROSS

2. A farm with crops and animals
6. Make full use of something
8. Has inputs, processes and outputs
9. The artificial watering of land
14. Something that can be used over and over again
15. Type of bog found on mountains
16. The production of crops

DOWN

1. Machine to scrape peat from top of bog
3. Machine used to drain bogs
4. What goes into the system
5. To decrease or reduce
7. Can be continued for a long time
10. Fish food
11. An amount you cannot exceed
12. Having an end
13. Land that is suitable for growing crops
15. Where peat is found

2 Economic Activities:
Focus on the secondary sector – Industry

○ I can explain what a secondary economic activity is and why it can be looked at as a system.

Review ●●● (/ /); Review ●●● (/ /); Review ●●● (/ /)

○ I can list and explain the factors that influence the location of an industry.

Review ●●● (/ /); Review ●●● (/ /); Review ●●● (/ /)

○ I can explain, giving examples, the difference between heavy, light and footloose industries.

Review ●●● (/ /); Review ●●● (/ /); Review ●●● (/ /)

○ I can explain the factors involved in the location of a heavy industry in Ireland.

Review ●●● (/ /); Review ●●● (/ /); Review ●●● (/ /)

○ I can explain the factors involved in the location of a light industry in Ireland.

Review ●●● (/ /); Review ●●● (/ /); Review ●●● (/ /)

○ I can explain how and why the location of industry has changed over time, and explain the term 'industrial inertia'.

Review ●●● (/ /); Review ●●● (/ /); Review ●●● (/ /)

○ I can explain the differences in the roles of women involved in manufacturing in developed and developing countries.

Review ●●● (/ /); Review ●●● (/ /); Review ●●● (/ /)

○ I can name and locate the three different industrial regions of the world.

Review ●●● (/ /); Review ●●● (/ /); Review ●●● (/ /)

○ I can name and describe the various impacts that industry can have on the environment.

Review ●●● (/ /); Review ●●● (/ /); Review ●●● (/ /)

○ I can explain, using an example, why local people can sometimes be in conflict with industry.

Review ●●● (/ /); Review ●●● (/ /); Review ●●● (/ /)

1. Define the following terms:

(a) Raw material

_____

_____

(b) Semi-finished product

_____

_____

(c) Finished product

_____

_____

(d) Manufacturing

_____

_____

2. List and explain the factors that influence the location of a factory, using the sample answer on raw material below as a guide.

(a) Raw material: factories may choose to locate close to the source of the raw materials they use. If the raw materials are big and heavy, it will be easier and cheaper to get them to the factory if they are nearby. If the raw materials are heavy, a factory may choose to locate near a port to make transport easier.

(b) Markets _____

_____

_____

(c) Transport facilities _____

_____

(d) Labour force _____

_____

_____

(e) Services _____

_____

_____

(f) Capital _____

_____

_____

(g) Government/EU policy _____

_____

_____

(h) Personal preferences _____

_____

_____

3. In your own words, define the following terms, giving examples of each:

(a) Heavy industry

_____

_____

_____

(b) Light industry

_____

_____

_____

(c) Multinational corporations (MNCs)

_____

_____

_____

(d) Footloose industry

_____

_____

_____

4. Explain two reasons why a factory might choose to locate in an industrial estate.

(a) _____

_____

_____

(b) _____

_____

_____

5. Heavy industry

Name of heavy industry	
Location	
Raw materials	
Process	
Output	
Transport	
Labour force	

6. Light industry

Name of light industry	
Location	
Output	
Transport	
Labour force	
Corporation tax	

7. Changing industrial location

(a) Why did the Industrial Revolution begin in Britain?

_____

_____

(b) What was the main source of energy before coal?

_____

_____

(c) Give two reasons why industry located close to coal mines during the Industrial Revolution.

_____

_____

(d) Give two reasons why coal was replaced by oil as an energy source.

_____

_____

8. Explain the term 'industrial inertia', giving an example you have studied.

_____

_____

9. Explain the difference between the developed world and the developing world.

_____

_____

10. Explain the difference in the role of women in industry under the following headings:

	Developed world	Developing world
The status of women		
Education		
Work and pay		

11. Define the following industrial regions, giving examples of countries in each region.

(a) Industrialised regions

_____

_____

(b) Newly industrialised regions

_____

_____

(c) Industrially emergent regions

_____

_____

12. How does acid rain form?

_____

_____

13. State and explain three problems associated with acid rain.

(a) _____

_____

_____

(b) _____

_____

_____

(c) _____

_____

_____

14. State and explain three ways to stop acid rain.

(a) _____

_____

_____

(b) _____

_____

_____

(c) _____

_____

_____

15. Describe and explain two positive and two negative aspects of incinerators.

Positive: _____

_____

Negative: _____

_____

_____

16. Word scramble

(a) Unscramble each of the clue words. The first one has been completed for you.

1. TICLAAP | C | A | P | I | T | A | L |

2. BUAROL FECOR   [□□□□□□₇] [□□□□□]

3. OOFOETOSL   [□□□□□□₆□□□]

4. BEXTAUI   [□□□□□□□]

5. LIEIRDSIDTAUSN   [□□□□□□□□□□□□□₃□]

6. ENRYCSAOD   [□₅□□□□□□□□]

7. TILMAINUATONL   [□□□□□□□□□□₁□□□]

8. TEKSARM   [□□□□□□□]

9. TCRUPDO   [□□□□₄□□□]

10. TONTRASRP   [□□□₂□□□□□□]

11. VETOENMNGR PYCOIL   [□□□□□□□□□□] [□□□□□□₈]

12. CAITSNERRONI   [□□□□□□□□□□□□]

(b) Copy the letters in the numbered cells to other cells below with the same number.

[□ □ □ □ □ □ □ □]
 1 2 3 4 5 6 7 8

3 Economic Activities:
Focus on the tertiary sector

○ I can explain why most people in developed countries work in the tertiary/service sector.

Review ●●● (/ /); Review ●●● (/ /); Review ●●● (/ /)

○ I can list examples of people working in the service industry.

Review ●●● (/ /); Review ●●● (/ /); Review ●●● (/ /)

○ I can explain why there has been a growth in tourism in recent years.

Review ●●● (/ /); Review ●●● (/ /); Review ●●● (/ /)

○ I can describe the four types of tourism in Ireland.

Review ●●● (/ /); Review ●●● (/ /); Review ●●● (/ /)

○ I can describe the factors that attract tourists to different places.

Review ●●● (/ /); Review ●●● (/ /); Review ●●● (/ /)

○ I can describe how tourism benefits a local economy.

Review ●●● (/ /); Review ●●● (/ /); Review ●●● (/ /)

○ I can describe the negative impacts of tourism on an area.

Review ●●● (/ /); Review ●●● (/ /); Review ●●● (/ /)

1. Why are fewer people employed in the tertiary sector in developing economies?

_____

_____

2. Giving examples of each, list four regions in Ireland that offer various attractions to tourists.

(a) _____

(b) _____

(c) _____

(d) _____

3. State and explain three reasons for the growth of tourism in recent years.

(a) _____

(b) _____

(c) _____

4. Choose a tourist attraction in Ireland with which you are familiar. Describe three reasons why this location attracts tourists.

Name	
Reason 1	
Reason 2	
Reason 3	

5. Tourism

(a) Name a tourist region outside of Ireland that you have studied.

_____

(b) Describe three factors of climate that attract tourists to this region.

_____

_____

_____

(c) Describe three other factors that attract tourists to this region.

_____

_____

_____

6. Name three ways tourism benefits the Spanish economy.

(a) _____

(b) _____

(c) _____

7. Describe three negative impacts of tourism in the European region you have studied.

(a) _____

(b) _____

(c) _____

8. Wordsearch

Find these words in the wordsearch below. Words can be vertical, horizontal, backwards or diagonal.

AFFORDABLE	AMENITIES	PEAK
FACILITIES	RESORT	MEDITERRANEAN
RECREATION	TEMPERATURE	CURRENCY
TOURISM	COMMUNICATION	ATTRACTIONS
EMPLOYMENT	TRANSPORT	

```
V F Y W A V G N I J O A W I A T P
J B Y U T A D O A H E D A H P D T
Q Q P U O U T E M P E R A T U R E
K K E H U E Z G U Q O A T I Y N X
M N A O R N I P C D M F T P F A J
C E K X I M B P I E P R R L Q E I
O L F M S E H U N K I F A E M N D
M B A A M N O I T A E R C E R A T
M A C I O U T S T Y R R T U I R R
U D I B N I S V R T Z M I Y T R A
N R L M E L E U G U C Y O E T E N
I O I S U F Y C U R R E N C Y T S
C F T V M S U D I Y E U S I Q I P
A F I E M P L O Y M E N T O U D O
T A E M P R L V O I V Z E D U E R
I W S A H L P U R T T T O C E M T
O P U E A R A X V R E S O R T D U
N C R K M P U I P U S F B S B I A
```

4 The Earth's Surface:
Shaping the crust

● I can name and identify the Earth's different layers.

Review ●●● (/ /); Review ●●● (/ /); Review ●●● (/ /)

● I can explain what plates are and how they move.

Review ●●● (/ /); Review ●●● (/ /); Review ●●● (/ /)

● I can explain what happens at each type of plate boundary.

Review ●●● (/ /); Review ●●● (/ /); Review ●●● (/ /)

● I can explain how volcanic activity occurs, giving an example of a volcano I have studied.

Review ●●● (/ /); Review ●●● (/ /); Review ●●● (/ /)

● I can list the three different types of volcano.

Review ●●● (/ /); Review ●●● (/ /); Review ●●● (/ /)

● I can explain the positive and negative effects of volcanoes.

Review ●●● (/ /); Review ●●● (/ /); Review ●●● (/ /)

● I can explain how earthquakes occur, giving an example of an earthquake I have studied.

Review ●●● (/ /); Review ●●● (/ /); Review ●●● (/ /)

● I can explain all the terms associated with the structure and measurement of earthquakes.

Review ●●● (/ /); Review ●●● (/ /); Review ●●● (/ /)

● I can describe the damage caused by earthquakes and how this damage could be reduced.

Review ●●● (/ /); Review ●●● (/ /); Review ●●● (/ /)

● I can explain the formation of fold mountains using examples from the different periods of folding I have studied.

Review ●●● (/ /); Review ●●● (/ /); Review ●●● (/ /)

1. Label the diagram.

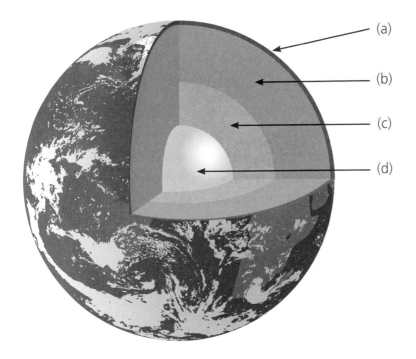

(a) _____

(b) _____

(c) _____

(d) _____

2. Define the following terms:

(a) Crust

_____

_____

_____

(b) Mantle

_____

_____

(c) Core

_____

_____

_____

(d) Plate

_____

_____

_____

(e) Plate boundary

_____

_____

_____

(f) Magma

_____

_____

_____

(g) Convection currents

_____

_____

_____

3. Explain the difference between a continental plate and an oceanic plate.

_____

_____

4. Label the diagram.

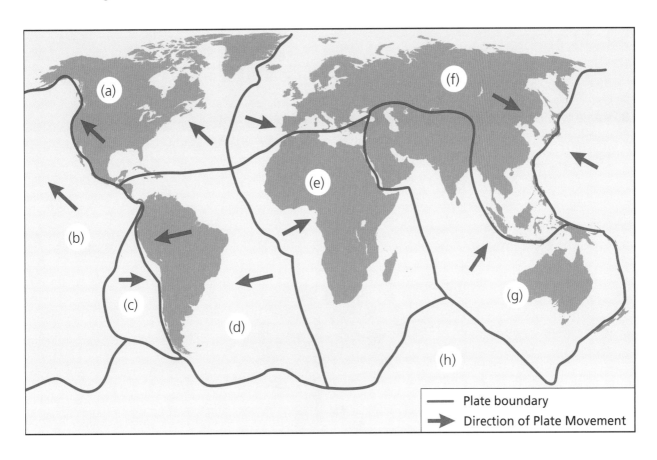

(a) _____   (e) _____

(b) _____   (f) _____

(c) _____   (g) _____

(d) _____   (h) _____

5. What happens at a destructive boundary? _____

_____

_____

6. What happens at a constructive boundary?_____

_____

_____

7. What happens at a passive boundary? _____

_____

_____

8. Name two regions in the world that have a lot of volcanic activity.

(a) _____

(b) _____

9. Label the diagram.

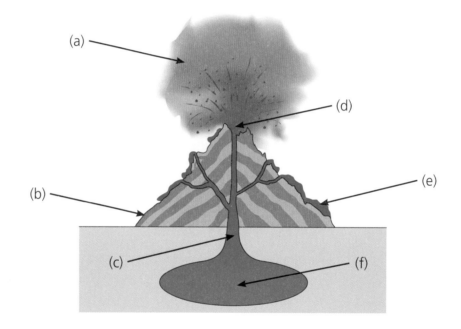

(a) _____

(b) _____

(c) _____

(d) _____

(e) _____

(f) _____

10. Name and explain the three different types of volcano.

(a) _____

(b) _____

(c) _____

11. 'Volcanoes have positive and negative effects.' Discuss this statement with reference to examples you have studied.

_____

_____

12. Describe the occurrence and impact of a volcanic eruption you have studied.

_____

_____

_____

13. Label the diagram.

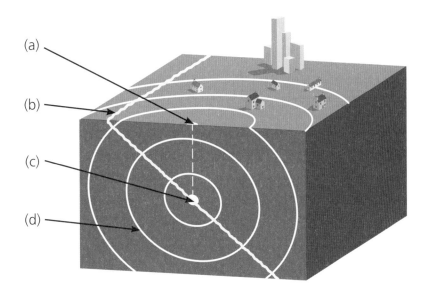

(a) _____   (c) _____

(b) _____   (d) _____

14. Explain the following terms:

(a) Earthquake

_____

_____

(b) Fault line

_____

_____

(c) Focus

_____

_____

(d) Epicentre

_____

_____

(e) Tremor

_____

_____

(f) Aftershock

_____

_____

(g) Seismograph

_____

_____

(h) Seismologist

_____

_____

(i) Richter scale

_____

_____

_____

15. Describe the occurrence and impact of an earthquake you have studied.

_____

_____

_____

_____

_____

16. Give an example of fold mountains that have occurred because of a continental and an oceanic plate colliding, naming the two plates involved.

_____

_____

17. Give an example of fold mountains that have occurred because of two continental plates colliding, naming the two plates involved.

_____

_____

18. Name two examples of fold mountains in Ireland formed during the Armorican period.

(a) _____

(b) _____

19. Try to sketch your own diagrams using these diagrams as a guide.

(a) Plates separating

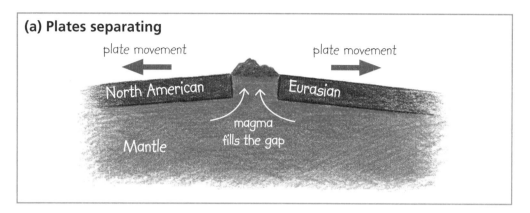

(b) Volcano

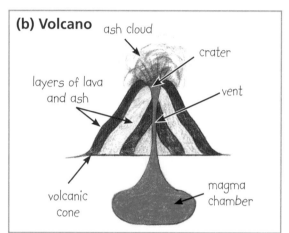

(c) Fold mountains

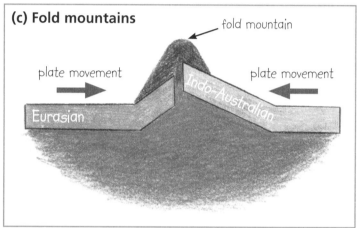

(d) Earthquake

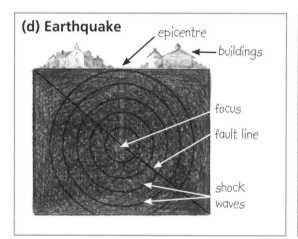

(e) Plates colliding

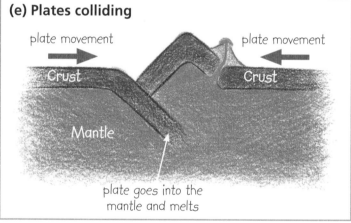

(f) The Earth

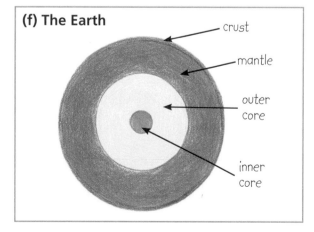

(g) Plates sliding by

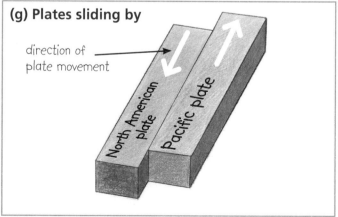

(a) Plates separating

(b) Volcano

(c) Fold mountains

(d) Earthquake

(e) Plates colliding

(f) The Earth

(g) Plates sliding by

5 Rocks:
How they are formed and used

⊙ I can classify rocks into three groupings: igneous, sedimentary and metamorphic.

Review ● ● ● (/ /); Review ● ● ● (/ /); Review ● ● ● (/ /)

⊙ I can describe the formation of two rocks within each group under these headings: formation, colour, texture, uses, and location.

Review ● ● ● (/ /); Review ● ● ● (/ /); Review ● ● ● (/ /)

⊙ I can explain how people use rocks.

Review ● ● ● (/ /); Review ● ● ● (/ /); Review ● ● ● (/ /)

1. Define the following terms:

(a) Hardness

_____

_____

(b) Texture

_____

_____

(c) Mineral content

_____

_____

2. Briefly explain in your own words how each of the following rock types are formed:

(a) Igneous rock

_____

_____

(b) Sedimentary rock

_____

_____

(c) Metamorphic rock

_____

_____

3. Name a county in which each of the rock types can be found:

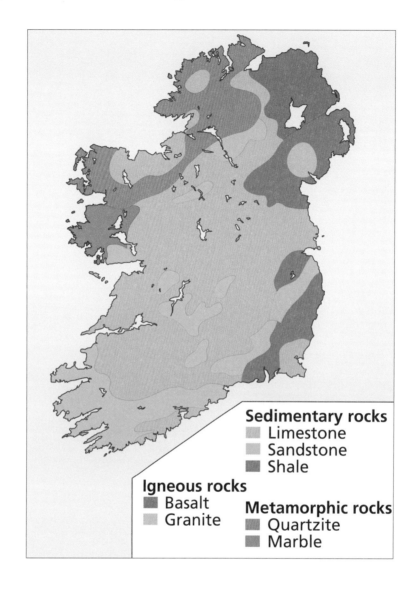

Sedimentary rocks
- Limestone
- Sandstone
- Shale

Igneous rocks
- Basalt
- Granite

Metamorphic rocks
- Quartzite
- Marble

(a) Basalt: _____

(b) Granite: _____

(c) Limestone: _____

(d) Sandstone: _____

(e) Shale: _____

(f) Quartzite: _____

(g) Marble: _____

4. Fill in this rock chart as you learn about igneous rocks in Chapter 5.

Two types of igneous rock		
Colour		
Texture		
Other characteristics		
Where it can be found in Ireland		
Economic uses		

5. Fill in this rock chart as you learn about sedimentary rocks in Chapter 5.

Two types of sedimentary rock		
Colour		
Texture		
Other characteristics		
Where it can be found in Ireland		
Economic uses		

6. What action does each arrow represent? Use the list to label the arrows seen on the diagram below.

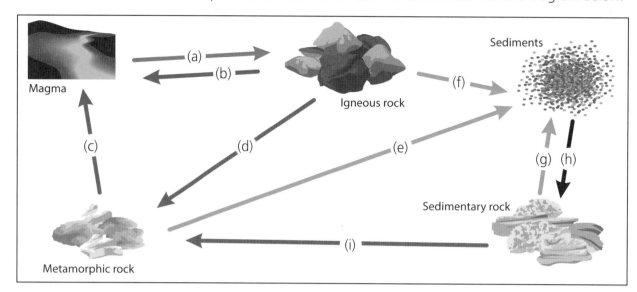

Weathering and erosion	(a) _____
	(b) _____
	(c) _____
Heat and pressure	(d) _____
Compaction and cementation	(e) _____
	(f) _____
Melting	(g) _____
Cooling	(h) _____
	(i) _____

7. Describe how people can use rocks for their economic benefit, using examples you have studied.

_____

_____

8. Why might people object to a quarry being opened near their community/home?

_____

_____

Denudation: 6
Weathering and erosion

- I can explain how the surface of the Earth is shaped by denudation, i.e. weathering and erosion.

  Review ●●● (/ /); Review ●●● (/ /); Review ●●● (/ /)

- I can explain the difference between weathering and erosion.

  Review ●●● (/ /); Review ●●● (/ /); Review ●●● (/ /)

- I can explain a type of mechanical/physical weathering.

  Review ●●● (/ /); Review ●●● (/ /); Review ●●● (/ /)

- I can explain a type of chemical weathering.

  Review ●●● (/ /); Review ●●● (/ /); Review ●●● (/ /)

- I can describe the formation of surface and underground landforms by chemical weathering.

  Review ●●● (/ /); Review ●●● (/ /); Review ●●● (/ /)

- I can discuss the impact that human activity has on the Burren.

  Review ●●● (/ /); Review ●●● (/ /); Review ●●● (/ /)

1. Define the following terms:

(a) Denudation

_____

_____

(b) Weathering

_____

_____

(c) Erosion

_____

_____

2. Name a type of mechanical weathering and explain with the aid of a labelled diagram how this type of weathering occurs.

Name: _____

Diagram

Explain: _____

_____

3. What is chemical weathering?

_____

_____

4. Name a type of chemical weathering and explain with the aid of a labelled diagram how this type of weathering occurs.

Name: _____

Diagram

Explain: _____

_____

_____

5. What is a Karst landscape? Give two examples of where this type of landscape can be found.

_____

_____

6. Explain, using the aid of a diagram and the DEPED formula, the formation of one surface feature you have studied that can be found in the Burren.

Name: _____

Description: _____

_____

Explanation: _____

_____

_____

_____

Processes: _____

_____

Example: _____

Diagram

7. Explain, using the aid of a diagram and the DEPED formula, the formation of one underground feature you have studied that can be found in the Burren.

Name: _____

Description: _____

_____

Explanation: _____

_____

_____

_____

Processes: _____

_____

Example: _____

Diagram

8. Who would be interested in visiting the Burren? List four examples.

(a) _____

(b) _____

(c) _____

(d) _____

9. Describe two arguments in favour of tourism in the Burren.

(a) _____

_____

_____

(b) _____

_____

_____

10. Describe two arguments against tourism in the Burren.

(a) _____

_____

_____

(b) _____

_____

_____

11. Wordsearch

Find these words in the wordsearch below. Words can be vertical, horizontal, backwards or diagonal.

BURREN	DIOXIDE	MECHANICAL	SCREE
CARBON	EXPANDS	PAVEMENTS	STALAGMITES
CARBONATION	FREEZE	PILLAR	UPLAND
CHEMICAL	HOLES	RAINWATER	WEAK
DENUDATION	LIMESTONE	REMOVAL	

```
Y  I  N  E  A  E  D  R  E  M  O  V  A  L  B  U  E
A  O  O  X  D  I  R  M  T  O  B  U  R  R  E  N  I
A  V  I  S  F  I  I  A  V  N  L  W  I  E  I  P  S
O  U  T  E  Q  R  X  D  E  N  U  D  A  T  I  O  N
M  O  A  T  I  U  E  O  S  G  P  N  B  H  B  O  U
P  N  N  I  I  R  O  E  I  N  A  S  N  M  B  D  C
Y  R  O  M  E  U  L  D  Z  D  Q  H  O  R  W  Y  D
Z  E  B  G  X  M  A  F  F  E  S  E  B  V  M  I  S
R  T  R  A  K  U  C  Y  T  E  V  D  R  E  E  Y  T
A  A  A  L  S  K  I  I  Y  O  O  N  A  D  C  E  N
L  W  C  A  D  E  M  G  R  X  V  A  C  O  H  W  E
L  N  A  T  N  T  E  K  B  M  S  L  M  I  A  E  M
I  I  T  S  A  D  H  R  G  I  P  P  O  I  N  A  E
P  A  R  P  P  E  C  S  C  M  O  U  R  U  I  K  V
N  R  E  S  X  I  R  A  K  S  F  E  C  R  C  E  A
E  H  O  A  E  L  I  M  E  S  T  O  N  E  A  R  P
T  M  Q  F  O  J  H  P  M  L  U  Y  X  I  L  D  R
H  O  L  E  S  Y  A  S  E  U  R  K  E  H  Y  Z  E
```

7 Introduction to Ordnance Survey Maps

Learning outcomes

- I can interpret scale on an Ordnance Survey (OS) map.

  Review ●●● (/ /); Review ●●● (/ /); Review ●●● (/ /)

- I can understand the national grid.

  Review ●●● (/ /); Review ●●● (/ /); Review ●●● (/ /)

- I can locate a position on an OS map using a four-figure grid reference.

  Review ●●● (/ /); Review ●●● (/ /); Review ●●● (/ /)

- I can locate a position on an OS map using a six-figure grid reference.

  Review ●●● (/ /); Review ●●● (/ /); Review ●●● (/ /)

- I can measure straight-line distance on an OS map.

  Review ●●● (/ /); Review ●●● (/ /); Review ●●● (/ /)

- I can measure curved-line distance on an OS map.

  Review ●●● (/ /); Review ●●● (/ /); Review ●●● (/ /)

- I can calculate regular area on an OS map.

  Review ●●● (/ /); Review ●●● (/ /); Review ●●● (/ /)

- I can calculate irregular area on an OS map.

  Review ●●● (/ /); Review ●●● (/ /); Review ●●● (/ /)

- I can use compass direction on an OS map.

  Review ●●● (/ /); Review ●●● (/ /); Review ●●● (/ /)

- I can identify the different ways in which height is shown on an OS map.

  Review ●●● (/ /); Review ●●● (/ /); Review ●●● (/ /)

- I can identify the differences between the types of slopes on an OS map.

  Review ●●● (/ /); Review ●●● (/ /); Review ●●● (/ /)

- I can draw a sketch map.

  Review ●●● (/ /); Review ●●● (/ /); Review ●●● (/ /)

Population:
Distribution, diversity and change

Learning outcomes

> I can identify the different stages of the population cycle.

Review ●●● (/ /); Review ●●● (/ /); Review ●●● (/ /)

> I can explain the factors that influence the rate of population change.

Review ●●● (/ /); Review ●●● (/ /); Review ●●● (/ /)

> I can account for the distribution of the world's population.

Review ●●● (/ /); Review ●●● (/ /); Review ●●● (/ /)

> I can identify the effects of high population densities and low population densities on social and economic geography.

Review ●●● (/ /); Review ●●● (/ /); Review ●●● (/ /)

> I can analyse a population pyramid and contrast the difference between developed and developing countries.

Review ●●● (/ /); Review ●●● (/ /); Review ●●● (/ /)

> I can explain why population pyramids are important.

Review ●●● (/ /); Review ●●● (/ /); Review ●●● (/ /)

> I can explain the differences in infant mortality rates and life expectancy between regions.

Review ●●● (/ /); Review ●●● (/ /); Review ●●● (/ /)

> I can explain reasons why people migrate (push and pull factors).

Review ●●● (/ /); Review ●●● (/ /); Review ●●● (/ /)

> I can explain the effects of an organised migration that I have studied.

Review ●●● (/ /); Review ●●● (/ /); Review ●●● (/ /)

1. Population growth

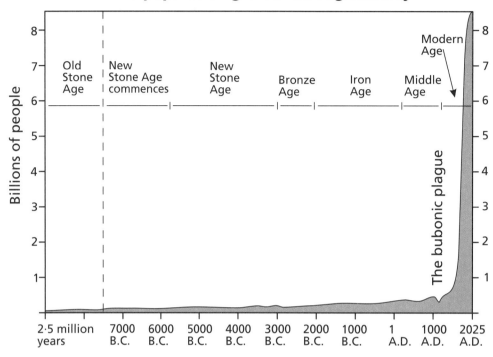

World population growth through history

(a) Give two reasons why the world's population has fluctuated throughout history.

_____

_____

(b) Explain the rapid population growth that has occurred since 1750.

_____

_____

_____

2. Explain the following terms:

(a) Birth rate

_____

_____

_____

(b) Death rate

_____

_____

_____

(c) Migration

_____

_____

_____

(d) Natural increase

_____

_____

_____

(e) Natural decrease

_____

_____

_____

3. The population cycle

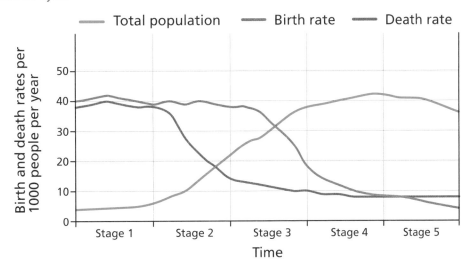

(a) Name each of the stages of the population cycle.

_____

_____

(b) Why are the birth rate and the death rate high in Stage 1?

_____

_____

_____

(c) What causes the death rate to drop in Stage 2?

_____

_____

_____

(d) Why is the population increasing rapidly in Stage 3?

_____

_____

(e) What causes population growth to slow down in Stage 4?

_____

_____

_____

(f) Why does the population go into decline in Stage 5?

_____

_____

_____

4. Name the factors that influence the rate of population change and write a statement to explain each one.

(a) Name: _____

Explanation:

_____

_____

_____

Development:

_____

_____

_____

(b) Name: _____

Explanation:

_____

_____

_____

Development:

_____

_____

_____

(c) Name: _____

Explanation:

_____

_____

Development:

_____

_____

_____

(d) Name: _____

Explanation:

_____

_____

_____

Development:

_____

_____

_____

(e) Name: _____

Explanation:

_____

_____

_____

Development:

_____

_____

_____

(f) Name: _____

Explanation:

_____

_____

_____

Development:

_____

_____

_____

5. What is the pessimistic view on population growth in the future?

_____

_____

_____

6. What is the optimistic view on population growth in the future?

_____

_____

_____

7. Define the term 'population distribution'.

_____

_____

_____

8. Define the term 'population density'.

_____

_____

_____

9. Read the case study on Brazil on pages 131–132 and answer the following questions:

   (a) What was the population of Brazil in 1500?

_____

   (b) Which European country colonised Brazil?

_____

   (c) Where did the colonists settle in Brazil when they arrived?

_____

   (d) What caused the population to grow at this time?

_____

   (e) Name the new Brazilian capital city, built in the 1960s.

_____

   (f) List three reasons why it has been difficult to develop the interior of Brazil.

_____

_____

_____

10. Read the case study on Ireland on pages 132–134 of the textbook and answer the following questions:

(a) Explain two reasons why the population of Ireland was high in 1840.

_____

_____

(b) What caused the Great Famine of 1845–1852?

_____

_____

_____

(c) Explain two immediate results of this famine.

_____

_____

(d) Explain two long-term effects of this famine.

_____

_____

(e) Explain two reasons for the rural depopulation of the west of Ireland today.

_____

_____

11. List five factors that attract people to live in certain regions.

(a) _____

(b) _____

(c) _____

(d) _____

(e) _____

12. Explain three reasons why so many people live in the Dublin region.

(a) Statement:

_____

Explanation:

_____

_____

_____

(b) Statement:

_____

Explanation:

_____

_____

_____

(c) Statement:

_____

Explanation:

_____

_____

_____

13. Compare and contrast the population distribution of the Northern Italian Plain (the Plain of Lombardy) and the Mezzogiorno under the following headings:

	Northern Italian Plain (Plain of Lombardy)	Mezzogiorno
Climate		
Relief		
Soils		
Minerals		
Economic activities		
Communications		

14. What information do population pyramids give us?

_____

_____

_____

15. Population pyramids: Brazil and Germany

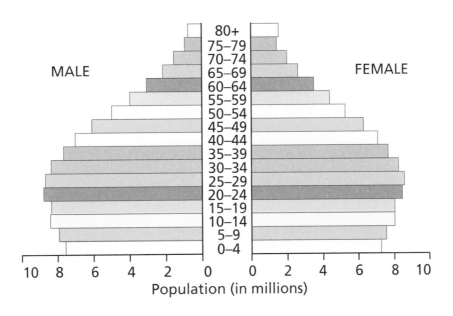

Brazil: 2010

MALE   FEMALE

80+
75–79
70–74
65–69
60–64
55–59
50–54
45–49
40–44
35–39
30–34
25–29
20–24
15–19
10–14
5–9
0–4

10 8 6 4 2 0   0 2 4 6 8 10
Population (in millions)

Germany: 2010

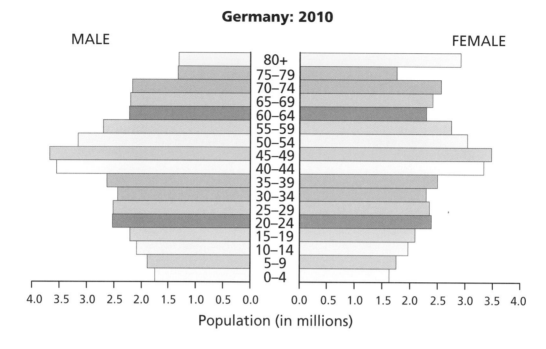

MALE   FEMALE

80+
75–79
70–74
65–69
60–64
55–59
50–54
45–49
40–44
35–39
30–34
25–29
20–24
15–19
10–14
5–9
0–4

4.0 3.5 3.0 2.5 2.0 1.5 1.0 0.5 0.0   0.0 0.5 1.0 1.5 2.0 2.5 3.0 3.5 4.0

Population (in millions)

(a) How many people are in the 0–4 age group in Brazil?

_____

(b) How many people are in the 0–4 age group in Germany?

_____

(c) Can you explain the difference in the two figures?

_____

_____

_____

(d) Is life expectancy higher in Brazil or Germany?

_____

(e) What evidence can be seen on the population pyramids to support your answer?

_____

_____

_____

(f) Explain why there is a difference in life expectancy between the two countries.

_____

_____

_____

16. Explain three reasons why population pyramids might be useful to governments and other agencies.

(a) _____

_____

_____

(b) _____

_____

_____

(c) _____

_____

_____

17. Fill in the table on population structure.

	City of high population density in the developing world	City of high population density in a developed country	Region of low population density in a developed country	Country with low population density in the developing world
Name				
Fact or figure (if available)				
Problem 1				
Statement				
Explain				
Problem 2				
Statement				
Explain				

18. Define the following terms:

(a) Infant mortality rate

_____

_____

_____

(b) Child mortality rate

_____

_____

_____

19. Explain three reasons why there are differences in the infant and child mortality rates between the north and south.

(a) _____

_____

_____

(b) _____

_____

_____

(c) _____

_____

_____

20. Explain three reasons why life expectancy is higher in the north than in the south.

(a) _____

_____

_____

(b) _____

_____

_____

(c) _____

_____

_____

21. Explain the following terms using examples you have studied:

(a) Internal migration

_____

_____

_____

(b) International migration

_____

_____

_____

(c) Push factors

_____

_____

_____

(d) Pull factors

_____

_____

_____

(e) Barriers to migration

_____

_____

_____

(f) Individual migration

_____

_____

_____

22. Describe three impacts of migration on the area left behind.

(a) _____

_____

_____

(b) _____

_____

_____

(c) _____

_____

_____

23. Describe three impacts of migration on the place to which people move.

(a) _____

_____

_____

(b) _____

_____

_____

(c) _____

_____

_____

24. Name an organised migration you have studied and describe three of its effects.

Name	
Effect 1	
Effect 2	
Effect 3	

25. Wordsearch

Find these words in the wordsearch below. Words can be vertical, horizontal, backwards or diagonal.

BALANCED	DEMOGRAPHY	IRRIGATION
BIRTHRATE	DEVELOPING	POLDERS
BUSTEES	DWELLERS	RAPID
CYCLE	FLUCTUATE	ROTATION
DEATHRATE	GLOBAL	SANITATION
DECLINE	IMPACT	TRANSITION

```
T  S  B  P  A  O  I  V  N  U  L  T  T  C  R  N  E
F  M  R  Q  C  V  U  I  S  P  D  O  C  H  A  N  P
E  N  I  L  C  E  D  Y  E  R  T  A  K  N  O  A  N
F  L  U  C  T  U  A  T  E  Y  E  R  G  I  C  O  I
C  P  N  O  I  T  A  T  O  R  C  L  T  E  I  Y  Y
T  P  A  T  B  T  V  K  G  A  H  A  L  T  U  E  H
E  T  A  R  H  T  A  E  D  P  G  M  A  E  O  C  P
O  D  C  Y  I  L  R  T  A  I  W  T  M  E  W  Y  A
E  E  A  T  Q  I  U  B  R  D  I  X  R  O  B  D  R
E  V  P  O  R  J  E  R  I  N  E  C  G  F  E  G  G
B  E  I  O  O  A  I  Y  A  R  I  C  N  X  D  E  O
A  L  C  R  L  O  N  S  T  E  T  M  C  U  E  C  M
L  O  O  O  S  D  E  S  H  H  T  H  P  Y  C  G  E
A  P  S  F  D  E  E  M  I  L  P  W  R  A  C  E  D
N  I  E  N  T  E  T  R  R  T  U  E  F  A  C  L  I
C  N  O  S  I  I  T  C  S  J  I  B  N  L  T  T  E
E  G  U  O  F  U  L  E  T  K  S  O  J  K  X  E  N
D  B  Y  C  G  L  O  B  A  L  U  W  N  M  E  A  E
```

9 Economic Inequality:
A world divided

I can identify the different types of countries and their economies.

Review ●●● (/ /); Review ●●● (/ /); Review ●●● (/ /)

I can describe the reasons for economic inequality between developed and less developed countries.

Review ●●● (/ /); Review ●●● (/ /); Review ●●● (/ /)

I can explain the exploitation of coffee-producing nations.

Review ●●● (/ /); Review ●●● (/ /); Review ●●● (/ /)

I can explain the different types of aid used to help developing countries.

Review ●●● (/ /); Review ●●● (/ /); Review ●●● (/ /)

I can account for the positives and negatives of giving aid to developing countries.

Review ●●● (/ /); Review ●●● (/ /); Review ●●● (/ /)

I can give an example of an Irish aid programme.

Review ●●● (/ /); Review ●●● (/ /); Review ●●● (/ /)

I can account for the obstacles to economic growth in a developing country.

Review ●●● (/ /); Review ●●● (/ /); Review ●●● (/ /)

I can explain the economic inequality in Ireland and in a European country.

Review ●●● (/ /); Review ●●● (/ /); Review ●●● (/ /)

I can describe the solutions to economic inequality.

Review ●●● (/ /); Review ●●● (/ /); Review ●●● (/ /)

1. Define the following terms using examples:

(a) Developed countries

_____

_____

_____

(b) Quickly developing countries

_____

_____

_____

(c) Slowly developing countries

_____

_____

_____

2. Explain the term 'Gross National Product' (GNP).

_____

_____

_____

3. Explain three reasons for the economic divide between developed and less developed countries.

(a) Reason:

_____

Explanation:

_____

_____

_____

(b) Reason:

_____

_____

_____

Explanation:

_____

_____

_____

(c) Reason:

_____

_____

_____

Explanation:

_____

_____

_____

4. Explain the term 'exploitation'.

_____

_____

_____

5. Explain three ways in which Ireland was exploited under British rule.

(a) _____

_____

_____

(b) _____

_____

_____

(c) _____

_____

_____

6. Name a commodity that is traded worldwide and a country that produces this commodity.

_____

_____

7. Explain three ways that countries from the developing world are exploited in trading this commodity.

(a) _____

_____

_____

(b) _____

_____

_____

(c) _____

_____

8. Explain the following terms using examples:

(a) Bilateral aid

_____

_____

_____

(b) Multilateral aid

_____

_____

_____

(c) Non-government organisations (NGOs)

_____

_____

_____

(d) Emergency aid

_____

_____

_____

(e) Development aid

_____

_____

_____

(f) Tied aid

_____

9. Explain three arguments in favour of giving aid.

(a) _____

_____

_____

(b) _____

_____

_____

(c) _____

_____

_____

10. Explain three arguments in favour of not giving aid.

(a) _____

_____

_____

(b) _____

_____

_____

(c) _____

_____

11. Read the case study on Ireland's aid programme on pages 180–182 and answer the following questions:

(a) Name the Irish programme for overseas aid.

_____

(b) Name a country to which the Irish government gives assistance. What is the population of that country?

_____

_____

(c) Briefly explain the work for food programme.

_____

_____

_____

(d) List three ways in which health and education are supported in this country.

_____

_____

_____

(e) How much of the budget is spent on combatting HIV/AIDS?

_____

(f) Why is 6% of the budget spent on governance issues?

_____

_____

_____

(g) Name two international organisations to which Ireland gives money for aid.

_____

_____

(h) Why did Ireland supply emergency aid to the Phillippines in 2011?

_____

_____

_____

(i) Name three Irish NGOs.

_____

_____

_____

12. With regard to a named example that you have studied, explain three obstacles to economic growth in developing countries.

Name: _____

(a) Obstacle: _____

Statement: _____

_____

Explanation: _____

_____

(b) Obstacle:

_____

Statement:

_____

_____

Explanation:

_____

_____

(c) Obstacle:

_____

Statement:

_____

_____

Explanation:

_____

_____

13. Name an economically developed region in Ireland and describe two reasons why it is a wealthy region.

_____

_____

_____

14. Name a less economically developed region in Ireland and describe two reasons why it is poor.

_____

_____

_____

15. Name an economically developed region outside of Ireland and describe two reasons why it is a wealthy region.

_____

_____

_____

16. Name a less economically developed region outside of Ireland and describe two reasons why it is poor.

_____

_____

_____

17. Describe and explain three steps that can be taken in order to balance economic inequality between rich and poor regions.

(a) _____

_____

_____

(b) _____

_____

_____

(c) _____

_____

18. Crossword

ACROSS

1. Richer countries are part of this world
2. One country taking over another
5. Giving farmers a fair price for their product
7. A voluntary organisation that helps people in the developing world
8. Owing money
10. Aid given through an organisation such as the UN
12. The wealth and resources of a country
13. Type of aid given after a disaster occurs

DOWN

1. Poorer countries are part of this world
3. Networks such as roads, rail and electricity
4. Dishonest behaviour by people in power for personal gain
6. Assistance given by rich countries to projects in poor countries
9. Widespread occurrence of an infectious disease
11. Aid given from one country to another

Mass Movement: 10
The movement of material down a slope

Learning outcomes

- I can explain what mass movement is.

  Review ● ● ● (/ /); Review ● ● ● (/ /); Review ● ● ● (/ /)

- I can list and explain the factors that affect mass movement.

  Review ● ● ● (/ /); Review ● ● ● (/ /); Review ● ● ● (/ /)

- I can identify the different types of mass movement.

  Review ● ● ● (/ /); Review ● ● ● (/ /); Review ● ● ● (/ /)

- I can discuss an example of mass movement that I have studied.

  Review ● ● ● (/ /); Review ● ● ● (/ /); Review ● ● ● (/ /)

1. Define the term 'regolith'.

_____

_____

_____

2. List and describe four factors that affect mass movement.

(a) _____

_____

_____

(b) _____

_____

_____

(c) _____

_____

_____

(d) _____

_____

_____

3. Explain the following terms:

(a) Soil creep

_____

_____

_____

(b) Bog burst

_____

_____

_____

(c) Mudflow

_____

_____

_____

(d) Landslide

_____

_____

_____

(e) Avalanche

_____

_____

_____

4. With reference to an example you have studied, explain the negative effects of a type of mass movement.

Question	Answer
Where did it happen? Include a map.	
When did it happen?	
Was this expected to happen?	
What were the causes (what made it happen)?	
What were the effects (what happened as a result)?	
What does the area look like now?	

5. Wordsearch

Find these terms in the wordsearch below. Words can be vertical, horizontal, backwards or diagonal.

AVALANCHE	LANDSLIDE	SATURATED	UNSTABLE
GRADIENT	MUDFLOW	SOIL CREEP	VEGETATION
GRAVITY	OVERGRAZING	TERRACETTE	
LAHAR	REGOLITH	UNDERCUTTING	

```
O E B O H O L O X W E I E S K N
P A D R I T I C W S I P G B F I
S N F I I I Y R T R Q K A K O R
R X O U L T O S B T U J V D G P
O E I I L S D N F G E O A E E E
M O G O T K D L A H A R L T U T
M U V O J A E N E N D S A A N T
O X D E L P T L A L E P N R D E
G U P F R I E E B L E T C U E C
R O F F L G T E G A N S H T R A
A E L X A O R H R E T U E A C R
V B W P C Y W A I C V S W S U R
I Q F I O H P D Z V L D N O T E
T T J S T E A C V I R I R U T T
Y R H D S R R T U C N F O E I P
T U K U G C K M F Q A G U S N D
O U R C E Z X T S D B F K R G N
```

11 Rivers:
Shaping our landscape

Learning outcomes

⊙ I can explain the common terms associated with rivers.

Review ●●● (/ /); Review ●●● (/ /); Review ●●● (/ /)

⊙ I can name and identify the three stages of a river.

Review ●●● (/ /); Review ●●● (/ /); Review ●●● (/ /)

⊙ I can describe the processes of river erosion.

Review ●●● (/ /); Review ●●● (/ /); Review ●●● (/ /)

⊙ I can describe the processes of river transportation.

Review ●●● (/ /); Review ●●● (/ /); Review ●●● (/ /)

⊙ I can explain how a river deposits its load.

Review ●●● (/ /); Review ●●● (/ /); Review ●●● (/ /)

⊙ I can explain in detail the formation of one feature of river erosion.

Review ●●● (/ /); Review ●●● (/ /); Review ●●● (/ /)

⊙ I can identify all features of river erosion.

Review ●●● (/ /); Review ●●● (/ /); Review ●●● (/ /)

⊙ I can explain in detail the formation of one feature of river deposition.

Review ●●● (/ /); Review ●●● (/ /); Review ●●● (/ /)

⊙ I can identify all features of river deposition.

Review ●●● (/ /); Review ●●● (/ /); Review ●●● (/ /)

⊙ I understand how humans interact with rivers in positive and negative ways.

Review ●●● (/ /); Review ●●● (/ /); Review ●●● (/ /)

1. Define the following terms:

(a) Source

_____

_____

_____

(b) Course

_____

_____

_____

(c) Confluence

_____

_____

_____

(d) Tributary

_____

_____

_____

(e) Mouth

_____

_____

_____

(f) Drainage basin

_____

_____

_____

(g) Watershed

_____

_____

_____

(h) Estuary

_____

_____

_____

2. Fill out the following on the different stages of a river:

> Upper or youthful stage	> Middle or mature stage	> Lower or old stage

3. Define the following terms:

(a) Erosion

_____

_____

_____

(b) Transportation

_____

_____

_____

(c) Deposition

_____

_____

_____

4. Name and describe the four processes of river erosion.

(a) _____

_____

_____

(b) _____

_____

_____

(c) _____

_____

_____

(d) _____

_____

_____

5. Name and describe the four processes of river transportation.

(a) _____

_____

_____

(b) _____

_____

_____

(c) _____

_____

_____

(d) _____

_____

_____

6. Explain four ways in which a river will deposit its load.

(a) _____

_____

_____

(b) _____

_____

(c) _____

_____

_____

(d) _____

_____

_____

7. Name three features of river erosion.

(a) _____

(b) _____

(c) _____

8. Using the DEPED formula, explain how one feature of river erosion is formed.

Name:

_____

Description:

_____

Explanation:

_____

_____

_____

Processes:

_____

_____

_____

Example: _____

Diagram

9. Name three features of river deposition.

(a) _____

(b) _____

(c) _____

10. Using the DEPED formula, explain how one feature of river deposition is formed.

Name: _____

Description: _____

_____

Explanation:

_____

_____

_____

Processes:

_____

Example:

_____

Diagram

11. List and explain three ways in which humans interact with rivers.

(a) _____

_____

_____

(b) _____

_____

_____

(c) _____

_____

_____

12. Explain two positive aspects of hydroelectric power (HEP).

(a) _____

_____

_____

(b) _____

_____

13. Explain two negative aspects of HEP.

(a) _____

_____

_____

(b) _____

_____

14. Wordsearch

Find these words in the wordsearch below. Words can be vertical, horizontal, backwards or diagonal.

ABRASION	EROSION	SEDIMENT	UNDERCUTTING
ALLUVIUM	HYDRAULIC	SOLUTION	VERTICAL
ATTRITION	INTERACTIONS	SUSPENSION	
DEPOSITION	LOAD	TRACTION	
DISCHARGE	SALTATION	TRANSPORTATION	

```
I  O  M  O  M  E  R  O  S  I  O  N  R  H  D  A  P  C
U  O  S  T  I  Y  W  G  Y  G  M  Y  M  E  D  D  E  Z
I  U  H  Y  D  R  A  U  L  I  C  P  P  E  B  D  F  S
N  O  I  T  U  L  O  S  E  C  N  O  C  O  D  R  A  N
A  S  A  L  T  A  T  I  O  N  S  O  G  A  I  E  D  O
D  S  H  I  S  W  F  U  E  I  L  N  H  U  F  A  E  S
I  F  I  N  O  I  T  A  T  R  O  P  S  N  A  R  T  N
S  M  D  T  N  E  M  I  D  E  S  O  R  O  P  U  A  O
C  O  R  J  L  F  O  A  B  R  A  S  I  O  N  U  L  I
H  N  O  I  S  N  E  P  S  U  S  I  M  D  T  J  L  T
A  L  A  C  I  T  R  E  V  T  O  R  E  R  N  X  U  C
R  F  G  B  O  S  S  O  E  C  U  R  A  S  B  D  V  A
G  N  L  N  I  P  D  L  N  Y  C  C  O  F  J  A  I  R
E  W  T  M  W  N  S  H  C  U  T  W  Y  D  N  O  U  E
E  D  G  A  T  T  R  I  T  I  O  N  E  D  R  L  M  T
O  L  P  U  E  O  H  T  O  U  U  I  I  W  C  A  H  N
Q  C  E  T  A  U  I  N  M  W  O  R  T  N  F  C  W  I
H  I  L  D  R  N  I  Z  E  N  C  G  R  O  U  Y  E  D
Z  R  C  M  G  P  O  Q  O  U  T  O  I  S  L  X  M  U
```

12 The Sea:
How it shapes our coast

> I can explain how waves are formed and how they shape the coastline.

Review ●●● (/ /); Review ●●● (/ /); Review ●●● (/ /)

> I can explain the difference between constructive and destructive waves.

Review ●●● (/ /); Review ●●● (/ /); Review ●●● (/ /)

> I can identify all features of coastal erosion.

Review ●●● (/ /); Review ●●● (/ /); Review ●●● (/ /)

> I can explain, with the aid of a labelled diagram, the formation of a feature of coastal erosion.

Review ●●● (/ /); Review ●●● (/ /); Review ●●● (/ /)

> I can explain longshore drift.

Review ●●● (/ /); Review ●●● (/ /); Review ●●● (/ /)

> I can identify all features of coastal deposition.

Review ●●● (/ /); Review ●●● (/ /); Review ●●● (/ /)

> I can explain, with the aid of a labelled diagram, the formation of a feature of coastal deposition..

Review ●●● (/ /); Review ●●● (/ /); Review ●●● (/ /)

> I can give examples of both positive and negative human interactions with the sea.

Review ●●● (/ /); Review ●●● (/ /); Review ●●● (/ /)

> I can explain, using examples, how humans try to protect the coastline from erosion.

Review ●●● (/ /); Review ●●● (/ /); Review ●●● (/ /)

1. Types of waves

Type of wave		
Diagram		
Description		
Causes erosion or deposition?		

2. Define the following terms:

(a) Fetch

_____

_____

_____

(b) Swash

_____

_____

_____

(c) Backwash

_____

_____

_____

(d) Constructive waves

_____

_____

_____

(e) Destructive waves

_____

_____

_____

(f) Hydraulic action

_____

_____

_____

(g) Abrasion

_____

_____

_____

(h) Compressed air

_____

_____

_____

(i) Solution

_____

_____

_____

(j) Attrition

_____

_____

_____

3. Name four features of coastal erosion.

(a) _____

(b) _____

(c) _____

(d) _____

4. Using the DEPED formula, explain how one feature of coastal erosion is formed.

Name: _____

Description: _____

_____

Explanation: _____

_____

_____

_____

Processes: _____

_____

Example: _____

Diagram

5. Using the DEPED formula, explain how one feature of coastal deposition is formed.

Name: _____

Description: _____

_____

Explanation:_____

_____

_____

_____

Processes: _____

_____

Example: _____

Diagram

6. Name two ways that people use coastal areas for their benefit. Explain each statement.

(a) Statement: _____

_____

Explanation: _____

_____

_____

Development: _____

_____

_____

(b) Statement: _____

_____

Explanation: _____

_____

_____

Development: _____

_____

_____

7. Describe two ways that people can have negative impacts on coastal areas.

(a) Statement: _____

_____

Explanation: _____

_____

_____

Development: _____

_____

_____

(b) Statement: _____

_____

Explanation: _____

_____

_____

Development: _____

_____

_____

8. Coastal management

Photograph	Name of coastal defence	How it works

Glaciation: 13
The work of ice

Learning outcomes

⊙ I can explain why an ice age occurs.

Review ●●● (/ /); Review ●●● (/ /); Review ●●● (/ /)

⊙ I can explain the processes of glacial erosion.

Review ●●● (/ /); Review ●●● (/ /); Review ●●● (/ /)

⊙ I can identify the features of glacial erosion.

Review ●●● (/ /); Review ●●● (/ /); Review ●●● (/ /)

⊙ I can explain the formation of one feature of glacial erosion.

Review ●●● (/ /); Review ●●● (/ /); Review ●●● (/ /)

⊙ I can identify the features of glacial deposition.

Review ●●● (/ /); Review ●●● (/ /); Review ●●● (/ /)

⊙ I can explain the formation of one feature of glacial deposition.

Review ●●● (/ /); Review ●●● (/ /); Review ●●● (/ /)

⊙ I can identify the features of meltwater deposition.

Review ●●● (/ /); Review ●●● (/ /); Review ●●● (/ /)

⊙ I can briefly explain the positive and negative impacts of glaciation.

Review ●●● (/ /); Review ●●● (/ /); Review ●●● (/ /)

1. What is an ice age?

_____

_____

_____

2. When did the last ice age end?

_____

_____

_____

3. Explain why an ice age occurs.

_____

_____

_____

4. Define the following processes of glacial erosion:

(a) Plucking

_____

_____

_____

(b) Abrasion

_____

_____

_____

5. List six features that are formed due to glacial erosion.

(a) _____   (d) _____

(b) _____   (e) _____

(c) _____   (f) _____

6. Using the DEPED formula, explain how one feature of glacial erosion is formed.

Name: _____

Description: _____

_____

Explanation: _____

_____

_____

_____

Processes: _____

_____

Example: _____

```
Diagram



```

7. Label the diagram with words from the box.

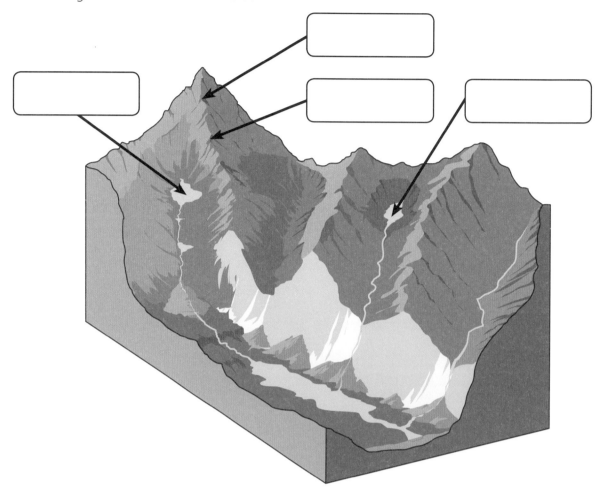

| Arête | Corrie | Tarn | Pyramidal peak |

Define the following words:

Arête: _____

Corrie (Cirque): _____

Pyramidal peak: _____

Tarn: _____

8. List three features of glacial deposition.

(a) _____

(b) _____

(c) _____

9. Using the DEPED formula, explain how one feature of glacial deposition is formed.

Name: _____

Description: _____

_____

Explanation:_____

_____

_____

_____

Processes: _____

_____

Example: _____

Diagram

10. Name two features formed as a result of glacial meltwater deposition.

(a) _____

(b) _____

11. Name and explain two ways in which glaciation has a positive impact on humans.

(a) _____

_____

_____

(b) _____

_____

_____

12. Name and explain two ways in which glaciation has a negative impact on humans.

(a) _____

_____

_____

(b) _____

_____

_____

13. Wordsearch

Find these words in the wordsearch below. Words can be vertical, horizontal, backwards or diagonal.

ABRASION	DRUMLIN	GRAVITY	PLUCKING
ACCUMULATION	ELLIPTICAL	LATERAL	STRIATIONS
AXIS	ERRATICS	MEDIAL	TERMINAL
BOULDER	ESKER	MORAINE	
COMPACTION	FJORD	ORBIT	
CREVASSE	GLACIATION	PATERNOSTER	

```
C I M E H T F I C O M P A C T I O N
R O I S C Q F U O P V U S O E E R L
F E H O N F I A W W L P Z A W E S A
T J R P M O R A I N E U A N K Q S C
U I O L A L I R E X S E C S W C F I
E O O R D T Y T B W S U E K I N F T
Y M G E D O E O A S T A V T I E H P
T L U L U S U R A I C L A B A N C I
I A S H A L I V N C R R A M H T G L
V P O U D C E X U O R T D T M X M L
A X K E E R I M A E S E S K E F O E
R M R I C E U A F G O T F J O R U Y
G E F T U L D O T A D M E A E L A H
O W F I A M U R N I Q N D R C V D L
G T S T W L I T U E O K D X N N O A
P T I C V K E X N M S N T I B R O A
E O A B R A S I O N L Q N W R M P O
N T E R M I N A L E K I L A I D E M
U F K E F U P V N Y M W N E E O I P
```

Learning outcomes

- I can identify the different drainage features formed by erosion and deposition on an OS map.

  Review ●●● (/ /); Review ●●● (/ /); Review ●●● (/ /)

- I can identify the different patterns of drainage on an OS map.

  Review ●●● (/ /); Review ●●● (/ /); Review ●●● (/ /)

- I can identify the features of coastal erosion and coastal deposition on an OS map.

  Review ●●● (/ /); Review ●●● (/ /); Review ●●● (/ /)

- I can identify the features of glacial erosion and glacial deposition on an OS map.

  Review ●●● (/ /); Review ●●● (/ /); Review ●●● (/ /)

- I can identify differences in height and its features on an OS map.

  Review ●●● (/ /); Review ●●● (/ /); Review ●●● (/ /)

Settlement and Communications: 15
Transport and where we live

Learning outcomes

- I can explain what attracts people to live in certain areas.

  Review ●●● (/ /); Review ●●● (/ /); Review ●●● (/ /)

- I can explain about a settlement from the past.

  Review ●●● (/ /); Review ●●● (/ /); Review ●●● (/ /)

- I can identify and explain the three groups of settlement patterns.

  Review ●●● (/ /); Review ●●● (/ /); Review ●●● (/ /)

- I can give an example of settlement on reclaimed land.

  Review ●●● (/ /); Review ●●● (/ /); Review ●●● (/ /)

- I can explain how the functions of a settlement can change over time.

  Review ●●● (/ /); Review ●●● (/ /); Review ●●● (/ /)

- I can explain how communication between settlements influences their development, using examples I have studied.

  Review ●●● (/ /); Review ●●● (/ /); Review ●●● (/ /)

1. List four needs that influence the location of settlements.

(a) _____

(b) _____

(c) _____

(d) _____

2. List four categories of settlements throughout history.

(a) _____

(b) _____

(c) _____

(d) _____

3. Can you list some antiquities or evidence from Celtic, Viking and Norman settlements that we might expect to see on the Irish landscape?

_____

_____

_____

_____

4. Name each type of settlement pattern and write a sentence to explain it.

(a) Name:

_____

Explain:

_____

_____

(b) Name:

Explain:

(c) Name:

Explain:

5. Label the different types of settlements seen in these diagrams.

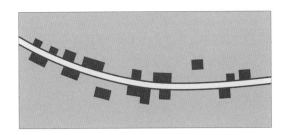

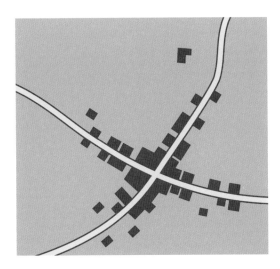

6. With the use of a named example, explain the term 'primate city'.

7. How has Christianity influenced the location of settlements? Give an example of one such settlement.

_____

_____

_____

8. How did the Vikings influence the location of settlements? Give an example of one such settlement.

_____

_____

_____

9. How did the Normans influence the location of settlements? Give an example of one such settlement.

_____

_____

_____

10. List four factors that influence the development of all nucleated settlements.

(a) _____

(b) _____

(c) _____

(d) _____

11. What are areas of reclaimed land called?

_____

12. Name a country where these can be found.

_____

13. Explain the following terms:

(a) The Zuiderzee project

_____

(b) Radial pattern

_____

(c) Overspill zones

_____

(d) Conurbation

_____

14. List seven functions of nucleated settlements and give a named example of each.

(a) Function: _____

Example: _____

(b) Function: _____

Example: _____

(c) Function: _____

Example: _____

(d) Function: _____

Example: _____

(e) Function: _____

Example: _____

(f) Function: _____

Example: _____

(g) Function: _____

Example: _____

15. Name a city whose function has changed over time.

_____

16. Explain three different functions that this city has had or has currently.

(a) _____

_____

_____

(b) _____

_____

_____

(c) _____

_____

_____

17. Read the case study on the different functions of Basel on pages 282–283 of your textbook and answer the following questions:

(a) What river is Basel situated on?

_____

(b) When did the Celts settle there and what did they build?

_____

_____

_____

(c) What led to its booming retail sector?

_____

_____

_____

(d) What is a nodal point? _____

_____

_____

(e) How did Basel's nodal point influence the growth of the city? _____

_____

_____

18. Using the table below, complete the Managing information and thinking / Working together section on page 283 of your textbook.

Name of town/city	
Past functions of the area	
Present functions of the area	

19. List four types of communication links.

(a) _____

(b) _____

(c) _____

(d) _____

20. Explain three projects that were part of the Government's Transport 21 Plan.

(a) _____

(b) _____

(c) _____

21. Explain the term 'satellite/dormitory town'.

_____

_____

_____

22. What are the high-speed trains in France called?

_____

23. What is the main form of transport in Paris called?

_____

24. Explain the term 'urban sprawl'.

_____

_____

_____

25. Pick an EU airport of your choice and find out its importance to its surrounding region. What benefits does it bring to the area?

Name of airport:	EU country:
Benefits to surrounding area:	

26. Crossword

ACROSS
4. Settlements in a line, e.g. along a road
5. To take something back
7. Having more than one function
9. A function that protects from attack
12. A city that is twice as big as the next biggest city
13. A town from which people commute to work

DOWN
1. The exchange of information or the transport links between places
2. Land in The Netherlands reclaimed from the sea
3. What a town is used for
6. Settlement which is scattered over a wide area
8. Settlements grouped together
10. In a group
11. A stretch of land and its physical features

16 Urbanisation:
The growth of towns and cities

- I can explain the development of an Irish city through the different periods of history.

  Review ●●● (/ /); Review ●●● (/ /); Review ●●● (/ /)

- I can identify, using an example, the functional zones of a city.

  Review ●●● (/ /); Review ●●● (/ /); Review ●●● (/ /)

- I can account for the intensity of land use and land values.

  Review ●●● (/ /); Review ●●● (/ /); Review ●●● (/ /)

- I can identify the different types of urban settlement.

  Review ●●● (/ /); Review ●●● (/ /); Review ●●● (/ /)

- I can account for the daily movement of people in an urban area.

  Review ●●● (/ /); Review ●●● (/ /); Review ●●● (/ /)

- I can explain the various urban problems that exist, using examples.

  Review ●●● (/ /); Review ●●● (/ /); Review ●●● (/ /)

- I can explain the solutions to urban problems such as urban renewal and urban redevelopment.

  Review ●●● (/ /); Review ●●● (/ /); Review ●●● (/ /)

1. Define the term 'urbanisation'.

_____

_____

_____

2. Read 'The growth of Dublin' on pages 294–295 of your textbook and answer the following
questions:

(a) Who first settled in Dublin and in what year?

_____

_____

(b) Name two structures built by the Anglo-Normans when they settled in Dublin.

_____

_____

(c) List three buildings in Dublin that were built during the Georgian period.

_____

_____

_____

(d) Explain what a tenement building was in nineteenth-century Dublin.

_____

_____

_____

(e) What is a satellite town?

_____

_____

_____

3. List and explain the five functional zones that are present in a city:

(a) Name:

_____

Explain:

_____

_____

_____

(b) Name:

_____

Explain:

_____

_____

_____

(c) Name:

_____

Explain:

_____

_____

_____

(d) Name:

_____

Explain:

_____

_____

_____

(e) Name:

_____

Explain:

_____

_____

_____

4. Label the diagram.

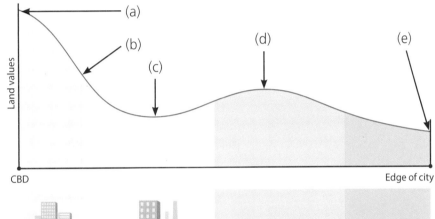

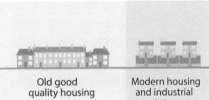

(a) _____

_____

(b) _____

_____

(c) _____

_____

(d) _____

_____

(e) _____

_____

5. Fill out the following examples of functional zones for the case study of London:

CBD, City of London	
Shopping area	
Residential area	
Industrial area	
Recreational area	
Shopping centre	

6. Identify the type of residential housing found in each photo.

(a) _____

(b) _____

(c) _____

(d) _____

7. Define the following terms:

(a) Commuters

_____

_____

_____

(b) Rush hour

_____

_____

_____

(c) Traffic congestion

_____

_____

_____

(d) Public transport

_____

_____

_____

8. List and explain two ways in which Dublin has tried to solve traffic congestion.

(a) _____

_____

_____

(b) _____

_____

_____

9. Name of urban area: _____

Measures to help reduce traffic congestion	How it will work

10. Define the following in relation to Dublin's urban problems:

(a) Zones of decline

_____

_____

_____

(b) Urban sprawl

_____

_____

_____

(c) Unemployment

_____

_____

_____

(d) Crime

_____

_____

_____

(e) Community disruption

_____

_____

_____

11. Describe the difference between urban renewal and urban redevelopment.

_____

_____

_____

12. Find an area in your local town or city that has undergone urbal renewal or redevelopment. Write a brief description of the area with your class and teacher. Describe what happened to the area and what existed before the redevelopment or renewal.

Name of area	
Description of the area	
Renewal or redevelopment	
What existed before	
What is present now	

13. In relation to a city in the developing world, describe four major problems that have resulted due to urbanisation.

City name:

_____

(a) Problem:

_____

_____

_____

(b) Problem:

_____

_____

_____

(c) Problem:

_____

_____

_____

(d) Problem:

_____

_____

_____

14. Wordsearch

Find these words in the wordsearch below. Words can be vertical, horizontal, backwards or diagonal.

ADMINISTRATIVE	FACILITIES	REDEVELOPMENT	SUBURB
COMMERCIAL	FOOTLOOSE	RENEWAL	TENEMENTS
COMMUTERS	FUNCTION	RESIDENTIAL	TERRACED
CONGESTION	GREENBELT	RURAL	ZONES
DECLINE	PATTERN	SANITATION	
DETACHED	RECREATION	SPRAWL	

```
I  S  C  O  G  D  S  P  R  A  W  L  D  E  T  A  C  H  E  D
M  T  O  Y  F  B  U  P  W  Z  X  T  E  R  R  A  C  E  D  U
Q  J  N  O  A  R  V  R  O  E  E  N  L  A  R  U  R  A  S  Z
R  D  G  A  D  M  I  N  I  S  T  R  A  T  I  V  E  R  Y  O
F  L  E  U  G  N  I  I  O  N  O  I  T  A  E  R  C  E  R  N
U  K  S  X  V  S  P  Y  S  I  F  O  O  T  L  O  O  S  E  E
N  E  T  W  K  O  O  I  O  N  X  S  F  X  O  Q  U  P  C  S
C  U  I  T  O  O  O  P  U  U  X  Y  L  N  C  A  E  D  O  I
T  M  O  N  I  S  H  O  R  M  F  O  T  Q  F  Y  E  U  A  G
I  F  N  A  K  X  V  S  T  N  E  M  E  N  E  T  D  S  E  H
O  H  N  W  Y  Z  N  Y  S  S  G  M  I  W  P  G  E  U  U  O
N  T  H  T  P  A  T  T  E  R  N  E  H  I  D  H  C  B  I  M
F  R  E  D  E  V  E  L  O  P  M  E  N  T  I  H  L  U  K  L
C  Q  N  F  M  Y  S  A  N  I  T  A  T  I  O  N  I  R  I  R
D  T  L  E  B  N  E  E  R  G  D  A  I  W  T  I  N  B  G  E
Z  T  X  C  T  W  Z  N  C  F  P  E  P  E  N  Y  E  E  O  N
V  Z  Y  R  P  F  M  P  R  R  O  Z  O  F  A  W  J  Z  O  E
C  O  M  M  E  R  C  I  A  L  C  P  C  D  T  U  F  P  N  W
S  R  E  T  U  M  M  O  C  F  A  C  I  L  I  T  I  E  S  A
R  E  S  I  D  E  N  T  I  A  L  H  X  A  H  K  E  F  B  L
```

Ordnance Survey Maps: 17
Reading the human landscape

Learning outcomes

⊙ I can identify and explain the reasons for rural patterns of settlement on an OS map.

Review ●●● (/ /); Review ●●● (/ /); Review ●●● (/ /)

⊙ I can identify and explain the history of settlement on an OS map.

Review ●●● (/ /); Review ●●● (/ /); Review ●●● (/ /)

⊙ I can identify and explain the reasons for location of settlement on an OS map.

Review ●●● (/ /); Review ●●● (/ /); Review ●●● (/ /)

⊙ I can explain the reasons for the development of settlement on an OS map.

Review ●●● (/ /); Review ●●● (/ /); Review ●●● (/ /)

⊙ I can identify the functions of a settlement through time on an OS map.

Review ●●● (/ /); Review ●●● (/ /); Review ●●● (/ /)

⊙ I can identify different land uses on an OS map.

Review ●●● (/ /); Review ●●● (/ /); Review ●●● (/ /)

⊙ I can locate the ideal site for various land uses on an OS map.

Review ●●● (/ /); Review ●●● (/ /); Review ●●● (/ /)

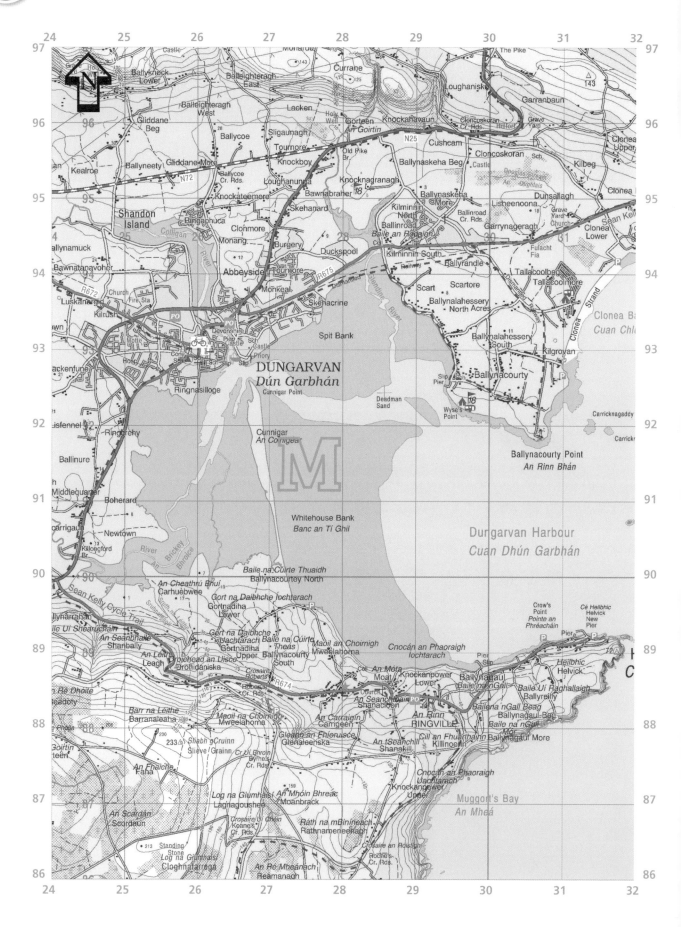

1. Get the four-figure grid reference for the following:

(a) Mixed woodland area

_____

(b) Clonea Strand

_____

(c) Townland area of Ballynacourty

_____

(d) A coniferous plantation

_____

2. Get the six-figure grid reference for the following:

(a) 18-hole golf course

_____

(b) Highest spot height on the map

_____

(c) A campsite

_____

(d) Boating activities

_____

3. Distance

(a) Measure the straight-line distance from the parking area at X 315 893 to the parking area at X 272 883.

(b) Measure the straight-line distance from the triangulation pillar at Slieve Grainn X 257 878 to the triangulation pillar at X 314 966.

(c) Measure the distance of the Sean Kelly cycle trail from X 241 899 to where it leaves the map extract at X 297 878.

(d) Measure the entire distance of the N72 on the map extract.

4. Direction

(a) If you took the cycle route from the centre of Dungarvan at X 258 930 and headed out along the R672, in what direction would you be heading?

(b) If you parked at the parking area at X 310 927 and walked along Clonea Strand to the parking area at X 318 942, in what direction would you be walking?

5. Give and locate three ways in which height is identified on this OS map.

(a) _____

(b) _____

(c) _____

6. What type of slope is located at X 27 96?

_____

7. Draw a sketch map of Dungarvan and include the following in your sketch:

   (a) A national primary road

   (b) A national secondary road

   (c) Sean Kelly cycle route

   (d) Clonea Strand

   (e) Urban area of Dungarvan

   (f) Area of land over 200 m

8. Locate the following features, formed along the course of a river:

(a) Tributary

_____

(b) Meander

_____

(c) Floodplain

_____

(d) V-shaped valley

_____

9. Locate the following features, formed as a result of coastal erosion and deposition.

(a) Sand spit

_____

(b) Headland

_____

(c) Beach

_____

(d) Cliff

_____

10. Locate and identify the three rural patterns of settlement on the OS map and explain why they have occurred.

(a) _____

_____

_____

(b) _____

_____

_____

(c) _____

_____

_____

11. 'This area has a long history of settlement.' Discuss this statement using three examples from the OS map.

_____

_____

_____

12. Explain, using examples, three reasons why Dungarvan developed at this location.

_____

_____

_____

13. Using the OS map, describe how the functions of Dungarvan have changed over time.

_____

_____

_____

18 Aerial Photographs:
A view from the air

‣ I can identify the different types of aerial photographs.

Review ●●● (/ /); Review ●●● (/ /); Review ●●● (/ /)

‣ I can identify what time of year an aerial photograph was taken.

Review ●●● (/ /); Review ●●● (/ /); Review ●●● (/ /)

‣ I can locate a position on an aerial photograph.

Review ●●● (/ /); Review ●●● (/ /); Review ●●● (/ /)

‣ I can draw a sketch map of an aerial photograph.

Review ●●● (/ /); Review ●●● (/ /); Review ●●● (/ /)

‣ I can identify urban land uses on an aerial photograph.

Review ●●● (/ /); Review ●●● (/ /); Review ●●● (/ /)

‣ I can identify rural land uses on an aerial photograph.

Review ●●● (/ /); Review ●●● (/ /); Review ●●● (/ /)

‣ I can identify transport issues on an aerial photograph.

Review ●●● (/ /); Review ●●● (/ /); Review ●●● (/ /)

‣ I can use both the aerial photograph and the OS map to compare information.

Review ●●● (/ /); Review ●●● (/ /); Review ●●● (/ /)

1. What type of photograph is this?

_____

2. What time of year do you think this photograph was taken and why?

_____

_____

3. Can you locate the following urban land uses on the photograph?

(a) Recreational

_____

(b) Residential

_____

(c) Industrial

_____

(d) Commercial

_____

(e) Tourism

_____

(f) Health

_____

(g) Ecclesiastical

_____

4. Locate and explain two ways in which traffic has been managed in the photograph.

_____

_____

_____

_____

5. Using the OS map of Dungarvan and the aerial photograph of Dungarvan, can you determine what direction the camera was facing when the photograph was taken?

_____

6. Draw a sketch map of the aerial photograph of Dungarvan and include the following:

(a) A residential area

(b) A recreational area

(c) Two bridges

(d) An industrial area

(e) Major routeway

7. It is proposed that a new shopping centre be built in the town. Where would you locate it? Give two reasons for your answer.

(a) _____

_____

_____

(b) _____

_____

_____

The Restless Atmosphere: 19
The heat engine

Learning outcomes

▸ I can explain the distribution of solar energy over the Earth's surface and within the atmosphere.

Review ●●● (/ /); Review ●●● (/ /); Review ●●● (/ /)

▸ I can explain the Earth's orbit around the Sun.

Review ●●● (/ /); Review ●●● (/ /); Review ●●● (/ /)

▸ I can explain the formation of weather fronts and how they cause variations in weather.

Review ●●● (/ /); Review ●●● (/ /); Review ●●● (/ /)

▸ I can identify and explain the different ways of measuring weather characteristics and the instruments used to do so.

Review ●●● (/ /); Review ●●● (/ /); Review ●●● (/ /)

▸ I can explain the water cycle.

Review ●●● (/ /); Review ●●● (/ /); Review ●●● (/ /)

▸ I can explain the greenhouse effect and how it is contributing to global warming.

Review ●●● (/ /); Review ●●● (/ /); Review ●●● (/ /)

1. List three gases present in the atmosphere.

(a) _____

(b) _____

(c) _____

2. Define the following terms:

(a) Stratosphere

_____

_____

_____

(b) Troposphere

_____

_____

_____

(c) Solar radiation

_____

_____

_____

3. What are the names of the two sections we can divide the Earth into?

_____

_____

4. What is the line that divides these two sections called?

_____

_____

5. What are the lines that measure distance from the equator called?

_____

_____

6. True or false?

(a) Air that heats and rises leaves an area of high pressure.

_____

(b) Winds blow from areas of high pressure to areas of low pressure.

_____

(c) The air that moves from the equator is cold air.

_____

7. Label the following:

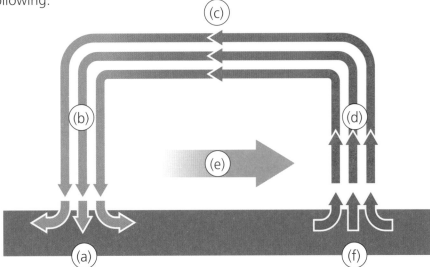

(a) _____

(b) _____

(c) _____

(d) _____

(e) _____

(f) _____

8. Explain the term 'Coriolis effect'.

_____

_____

_____

9. Label each current and say whether it is cold or warm.

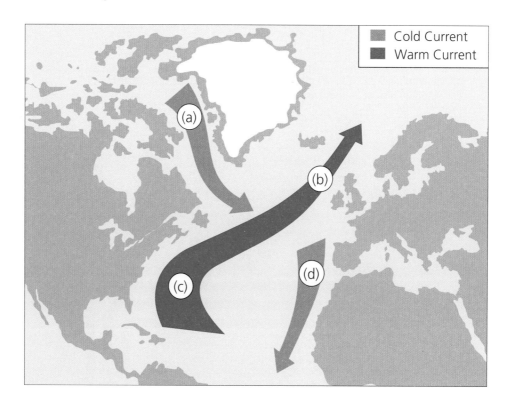

(a) _____

(b) _____

(c) _____

(d) _____

10. Explain the term 'air masses' and give three examples.

_____

_____

_____

11. Explain the following terms:

(a) Isobars

_____

_____

_____

(b) Fronts

_____

_____

_____

(c) Millibars

_____

_____

_____

12. Define the following terms:

(a) Warm front

_____

_____

_____

(b) Cold front

_____

_____

_____

(c) Occuluded front

_____

_____

_____

(d) Anticyclone

_____

_____

_____

(e) Depression

_____

_____

_____

13. List the seven characteristics of weather that are measured constantly.

(a) _____

(b) _____

(c) _____

(d) _____

(e) _____

(f) _____

(g) _____

14. What is the name of the person who prepares the weather forecast?

_____

15. Why is the weather forecast important to us?

_____

_____

_____

16. What is the name of the meteorological service in Ireland?

_____

17. What are synoptic maps?

_____

_____

_____

18. Fill in the table. Begin by naming the instruments and what they measure.

Instrument					
What it measures					
Unit of measurement					
How it is shown on a synoptic map					

19. Label each cloud type.

(a) _____

(b) _____

(c) _____

20. Explain the term 'convectional rain' with the aid of a diagram.

_____

_____

_____

_____

_____

_____

_____

_____

Diagram

21. Label the diagram using the following terms: warm air, condenses, relief rain, rain shadow.

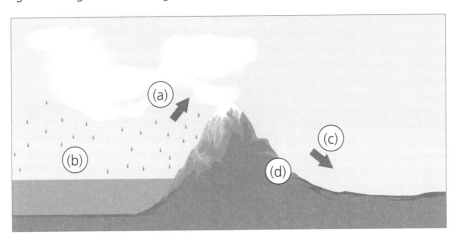

(a) _____

(b) _____

(c) _____

(d) _____

22. Label the stages of the water cycle.

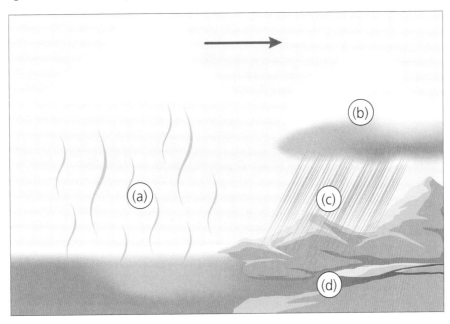

(a) _____

(b) _____

(c) _____

(d) _____

23. Explain the terms you have labelled on the diagram in question 22.

(a) _____

(b) _____

(c) _____

(d) _____

24. Draw a diagram illustrating the greenhouse effect.

Diagram

25. Explain two actions that people can take to reduce the greenhouse effect.

(a) _____

(b) _____

26. Wordsearch

Find these words in the wordsearch below. Words can be vertical, horizontal, backwards or diagonal.

ANEMOMETER	CURRENTS	HUMIDITY	PRESSURE
ANTICYCLONE	ENERGY	ISOBARS	SOLAR
ASCENDING	DEPRESSION	ISOHELS	SPHERICAL
ATMOSPHERE	DESCENDING	LATITUDE	RADIATION
CONVECTION	DOLDRUMS	ORBIT	TROPOSPHERE
CORIOLIS	FRONTS	PRECIPITATION	

```
S  E  N  A  U  D  J  F  C  T  A  O  A  D  S  F  D  L  U  T
J  O  Q  E  S  C  E  A  I  B  F  S  A  F  L  C  C  A  A  R
G  Y  L  R  O  G  N  B  P  O  R  I  N  U  E  R  E  H  T  O
S  E  U  A  W  T  R  A  A  A  O  K  E  N  H  E  R  U  M  P
C  P  S  Y  R  O  T  F  B  K  N  C  M  O  O  I  U  M  O  O
R  M  P  K  W  V  A  O  G  V  T  U  O  Y  S  V  C  I  S  S
C  S  H  N  Z  O  S  R  F  D  S  X  M  R  I  E  O  D  P  P
P  W  E  A  O  I  C  S  N  O  O  H  E  L  I  A  K  I  H  H
R  D  R  G  N  I  D  N  E  C  S  A  T  E  C  O  O  T  E  E
E  E  I  R  Y  T  T  U  R  F  E  U  E  N  U  G  L  Y  R  R
C  G  C  A  M  J  I  C  K  V  C  T  R  E  R  M  D  I  E  E
I  N  A  D  P  P  I  C  E  T  E  K  D  R  R  D  E  L  S  E
P  I  L  I  B  C  S  E  Y  V  J  R  A  G  E  O  P  A  E  T
I  D  N  A  A  E  W  Y  V  C  N  U  F  Y  N  L  R  T  P  D
T  N  L  T  I  S  Y  M  A  M  L  O  R  Y  T  D  E  I  R  Y
A  E  W  I  O  N  Y  V  P  D  I  O  C  G  S  R  S  T  T  E
T  C  O  O  P  R  E  S  S  U  R  E  N  O  X  U  S  U  A  D
I  S  W  N  R  H  A  O  O  L  Z  D  R  E  E  M  I  D  T  Z
O  E  P  O  I  N  K  T  N  K  F  N  E  N  A  S  O  E  S  M
N  D  N  I  S  U  G  N  D  N  T  O  D  M  E  V  N  W  Z  N
```

20 Climates:
Identifying and classifying climate types

I can explain what factors influence climates.

Review ● ● ● (/ /); Review ● ● ● (/ /); Review ● ● ● (/ /)

I can recognise different climate types.

Review ● ● ● (/ /); Review ● ● ● (/ /); Review ● ● ● (/ /)

I can explain how climates influence natural regions.

Review ● ● ● (/ /); Review ● ● ● (/ /); Review ● ● ● (/ /)

I can give examples of hot climates, temperate climates and cold climates and explain characteristics of each.

Review ● ● ● (/ /); Review ● ● ● (/ /); Review ● ● ● (/ /)

I can explain how climates influence human activity.

Review ● ● ● (/ /); Review ● ● ● (/ /); Review ● ● ● (/ /)

I can explain how humans have aided in causing desertification and deforestation.

Review ● ● ● (/ /); Review ● ● ● (/ /); Review ● ● ● (/ /)

1. Explain the difference between weather and climate.

_____

_____

_____

2. List and explain three factors that influence climate.

(a) _____

_____

_____

(b) _____

_____

_____

(c) _____

_____

_____

3. Can you explain why it is colder at (a) than at (b)?

_____

_____

_____

4. Explain why it is colder in Zurich than in Dublin in the winter.

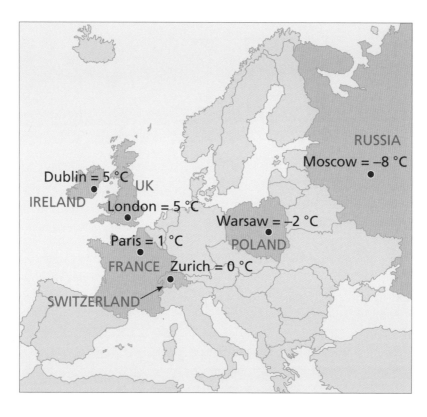

_____

_____

_____

_____

_____

5. Explain the term 'prevailing winds' and name Ireland's prevailing winds.

_____

_____

6. Why are the easterly winds that blow over Ireland cold in the winter and warm in the summer?

_____

_____

_____

_____

7. Explain the following terms:

(a) Aspect

_____

(b) Altitude

_____

8. Can you explain why it is colder at (a) than at (b)?

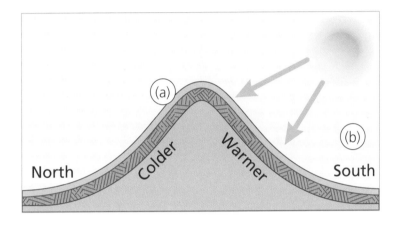

_____

_____

_____

9. What is a natural region?

_____

_____

_____

10. Name the four layers of vegetation in a rainforest.

(a) _____

(b) _____

(c) _____

(d) _____

11. Fill in the table as you learn about each type of climate.

Climate Type	Location	Temperature	Rainfall	Soil	Natural Vegetation	Wildlife	Human Activity
Equatorial Climate							
Savannah Climate							
Hot Desert Climate							
Cool Temperate Oceanic Climate							
Warm Temperate Oceanic Climate							
Boreal Climate							
Tundra Climate							

12. Equatorial climate

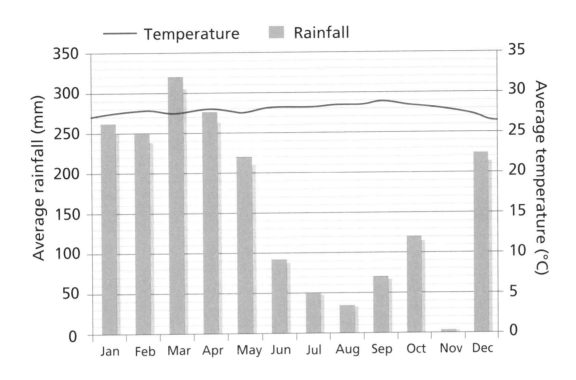

(a) What was the average rainfall in March?

_____

(b) What was the average rainfall in September?

_____

(c) What was the mean average rainfall for the first three months of the year?

_____

(d) What was the total rainfall for June, July and August?

_____

(e) Explain why there was little variation in the temperature throughout the year.

_____

_____

_____

13. Explain three positive impacts of clearing the rainforests.

(a) _____

_____

(b) _____

_____

(c) _____

_____

14. Explain three negative impacts of clearing the rainforests.

(a) _____

_____

(b) _____

_____

(c) _____

_____

15. Explain the following terms:

(a) Deforestation

_____

_____

(b) Soil erosion

_____

_____

(c) Shifting cultivation

_____

_____

16. Savannah climate

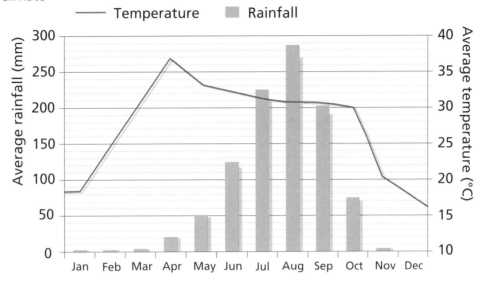

(a) Which month had the highest temperature?

_____

(b) What was the average temperature in September?

_____

(c) What was the mean monthly rainfall for June, July and August?

_____

17. Examine this diagram. Name four countries that have hot desert regions.

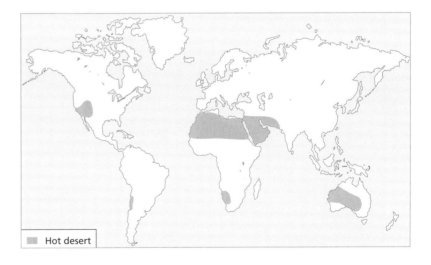

(a) _____

(b) _____

(c) _____

(d) _____

18. Explain two ways that vegetation has adapted to survive hot desert conditions.

(a) _____

_____

(b) _____

_____

19. Explain two ways that animals have adapted to survive hot desert conditions.

(a) _____

_____

(b) _____

_____

20. Name a tourist region you have studied. In relation to that region, list two advantages of tourism and two disadvantages of tourism.

Tourist region:	Country:
Advantages of tourism	Disadvantages of tourism

21. Explain two ways that vegetation has adapted to survive cold climatic conditions.

(a) _____

_____

(b) _____

_____

22. Explain two ways that animals have adapted to survive cold climatic conditions.

(a) _____

(b) _____

23. Crossword

ACROSS
4. Uncovered or unprotected
7. Type of climates in mid-latitudes
9. When something is capable of being continued
12. The tribe that live on the Masai Mara
13. Type of holiday in savannah regions
15. A fertile area in a desert

DOWN
1. Plants or animals that come out at night
2. Common winds
3. Height above sea level
5. To change or adjust to certain conditions
6. The spreading of the desert
8. Distance north or south of the equator
10. Plants that are able to store water
11. Originating or occurring naturally in a particular place
14. The direction a place faces

21 Soil:
A vital natural resource

Learning outcomes

- I can explain what soil is, how it is formed and what it is made of.

  Review ●●● (/ /); Review ●●● (/ /); Review ●●● (/ /)

- I can explain about the different types of soils and their individual profiles.

  Review ●●● (/ /); Review ●●● (/ /); Review ●●● (/ /)

- I can explain the characteristics of two Irish soil types and of tropical red soils.

  Review ●●● (/ /); Review ●●● (/ /); Review ●●● (/ /)

- I can explain how soil influences vegetation and vegetation influences soil.

  Review ●●● (/ /); Review ●●● (/ /); Review ●●● (/ /)

1. Label each section in the pie chart with the ingredients of soils and the percentage (%) of each ingredient.

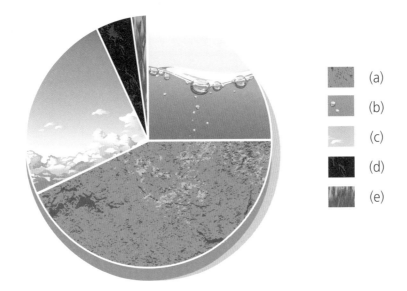

(a) _____

(b) _____

(c) _____

(d) _____

(e) _____

2. Circle the correct term in brackets in the statements below.

(a) The main ingredient in soils is (living organisms / mineral matter).

(b) Air containing (nitrogen / carbon dioxide) is vital for living organisms in the soil to survive.

(c) Water makes up about (25% / 20%) of soil.

(d) Humus is a (dark / light) jelly-like substance.

(e) Humus provides the soils with (nutrients / dissolved minerals).

3. What is the term used to describe the washing of minerals through soil?

_____

4. The build-up of minerals at the bottom of the A Horizon is called the _____.

5. In the space provided, draw and label a soil profile. Explain the following terms:

(a) Top soil

_____

(b) Horizon

_____

(c) Bedrock

_____

Diagram

6. Choose two factors from the list below and explain how they influence soil formation: climate, parent material, time, living organisms, landscape, vegetation.

(a) _____

_____

(b) _____

_____

7. List four different Irish soil types and fill in the table on the following page.

(a) _____

(b) _____

(c) _____

(d) _____

Soil Type	Location	How it was formed	Is there much humus?	Is it fertile?	Is it well drained?	Does leaching occur?	Is it good for agriculture?
Brown Earth Soils							
Podzol Soils							
Gley Soils							
Peaty Soils							
Tropical Red Soils							

8. Fill in the table below, explaining how each factor influences both soil and vegetation.

Factor	Influence on soil	Influence on vegetation
Fertility		
Plant litter		
Soil erosion		
Leaching		
Waterlogging		
Nutrients		

9. Explain two major effects of deforestation.

(a) _____

_____

(b) _____

_____

10. Explain how each of the following has a negative impact on soils:

(a) Over cropping

_____

_____

(b) Monoculture

_____

_____

(c) Overgrazing

_____

_____

11. Wordsearch

Find these words in the wordsearch below. Words can be vertical, horizontal, backwards or diagonal.

AIR	HARDPAN	MONOCULTURE	PODZOL
BACTERIA	HORIZONS	NITROGEN	PROFILE
BEDROCK	HUMUS	ORGANISMS	SILT
DEFORESTATION	LEACHING	OVERCROPPING	VEGETATION
FUNGI	LITTER	OVERGRAZING	WATER
GLEY	MINERALS	OXYGEN	WATERLOGGED

```
O  U  U  P  O  O  C  F  I  N  T  X  S  Q  A  R  W  J  R
V  I  P  U  F  S  S  E  D  W  N  J  T  A  A  I  R  C
E  P  O  D  Z  O  L  G  E  K  K  T  X  L  O  M  O  I  I
R  Y  N  I  B  J  O  O  K  N  L  D  L  I  V  S  O  G  I
C  N  Q  V  M  R  L  O  R  G  A  N  I  S  M  S  O  N  T
R  I  F  C  T  S  I  L  V  E  M  Y  W  H  M  F  V  U  P
O  L  A  I  S  I  T  O  E  R  S  O  A  F  I  N  E  F  H
P  H  N  C  G  Z  T  U  G  U  G  M  T  X  N  O  R  U  A
P  O  R  O  B  X  E  W  E  T  S  T  E  B  E  I  G  E  R
I  R  K  J  T  D  R  A  T  L  Z  X  R  G  R  T  R  R  D
N  I  C  A  E  I  R  T  A  U  J  N  S  Y  A  A  A  G  P
G  Z  O  I  L  F  E  E  T  C  L  E  E  A  L  T  Z  N  A
M  O  R  H  I  U  J  R  I  O  T  P  T  I  S  S  I  I  N
P  N  D  Y  F  T  I  L  O  N  R  X  A  R  M  E  N  H  R
Z  S  E  S  O  S  E  O  N  O  N  E  O  E  P  R  G  C  R
V  L  B  W  R  N  G  G  E  M  K  E  A  T  Y  O  E  A  Y
G  U  C  F  P  O  T  G  G  F  C  T  T  C  Y  F  R  E  U
S  N  E  G  Y  X  O  E  H  U  M  U  S  A  R  E  P  L  O
V  C  E  S  R  K  X  D  D  M  T  R  M  B  T  D  F  T  T
```

Notes